Shortcuts to Success

Maths
for Leaving Certificate Ordinary Level

Carl Lynch

GILL & MACMILLAN

Gill & Macmillan Ltd
Hume Avenue
Park West
Dublin 12
with associated companies throughout the world
www.gillmacmillan.ie

© Carl Lynch 2006
13-digit ISBN: 978 0 7171 3998 9
10-digit ISBN: 0 7171 3998 0

Typeset in Replika Press Pvt Ltd

The paper used in this book is made from the wood pulp of managed forests. For every tree felled, at least one tree is planted, thereby renewing natural resources.

All rights reserved.
No part of this publication may be copied, reproduced or transmitted in any form or by any means without written permission of the publishers or else under the terms of any licence permitting limited copying issued by the Irish Copyright Licensing Agency.

Contents

		Page
	Introduction	v

Paper I

Chapter 1	Ratios, Percentage and Tax	1
Chapter 2	Algebra	16
Chapter 3	Complex Numbers	35
Chapter 4	Sequences and Series	42
Chapter 5	Calculus and Differentiation	50
Chapter 6	Functions and Graphs	62

Paper II

Chapter 7	Area and Volume	69
Chapter 8	The Line	85
Chapter 9	The Circle	95
Chapter 10	Theorems and Enlargements	104
Chapter 11	Trigonometry	111
Chapter 12	Probability	124
Chapter 13	Statistics	132
Chapter 14	Linear Programming	144

Introduction
Pass Maths

The aim of this book is to cover the whole Leaving Cert course, making it as easy as possible to understand. No textbook on its own can guarantee that you achieve your best grade; you must put in the right kind of work yourself. No matter how good or bad you are at maths, you need to put in time and effort.

Resource material

There are places where you may obtain help in order to understand the material:

(i) from class notes
(ii) from the textbooks
(iii) from this revision book.

Revision

This should take a very set format, which you should stick to in the order below.

Step 1:	Make sure you understand the material covered.
Step 2:	**LEARN** off methods and formulae.
Step 3:	Do Leaving Cert questions in **20** minutes.

How to use these notes to help you with revision

Each night, try to do some revision before you do homework, even if only for 10 minutes.

When you use this book you should have a hardback notebook and a rough-work copy. Start with the chapter you find easy in school, then do a hard one, and so on.

Write down the headings in your hardback. Under each heading write down the method and any formulae that you need to learn. Try to be active when doing this, i.e. try to remember what you have written.

By the end of the year you will have created your own set of notes that you will be able to use to learn basic facts. If you find you cannot remember the formulae, then you have to write them out over and over until they stick in your mind.

Under each heading in this book there are examples; you should go through the solutions to see whether you can work them out for yourself (in the rough-book copy). This is the most important idea of all, as working out questions is the only real way to improve. If you are struggling, there are detailed explanations with nearly every example to help you through.

Homework

When you do your written homework you should really treat it as a test, i.e. take out the homework and a blank page and without looking at notes see whether you can do the work.

Evaluation

After Christmas start to figure out where you are at and keep doing this every two weeks or so. On the back page of your maths copy write down headings and fill in each section of the course.

know   maybe know   do not know

When you have identified the material that you do not know, then these are the areas in which to put more and more effort.

Ideally before the Leaving Cert you want everything to be in the 'know' list, but this might not happen. Make sure that you have 6 questions from both papers that you are somewhat confident with and especially some knowledge of algebra (no matter how basic).

The course can also be generally broken down according to how difficult it is, as perceived by students. Here is how I would break it up. We are all different and some of you will like different chapters from others, so this is only a rough guideline.

Easy	*Not so easy*	*Harder*
Money	Differentiation	Algebra
Complex numbers	Area and volume	Sequences and series
Statistics	Line	Circle
Linear programming	Probability	Trigonometry
		Theorems

Make out your own list and if you are really struggling, put a lot of effort into the easier ones, as these are the ones you can do and therefore will pick up marks in.

Examination

Here are the steps to follow in the Leaving Cert (you should try to practise these when doing school exams):

Step 1: Read the whole paper. Some see this as a waste of time, but to me it is vital for two reasons.
  (i) You can pick out the parts you can do.
  (ii) You start to think about each part you cannot do. Remember, when you first read the paper it looks much harder than it really is.

Step 2: Do your best question first.

Step 3: READ the question before you start; if you get stuck halfway down READ the question again.

Step 4: When you are finished READ the question, to make sure you have answered all parts.

Step 5: Stick to the time. You will have time at the end to fill in the gaps and check answers.

Do not get sucked in and spend too much time on any one part, or time trying to get an answer out.

You will make mistakes and you will start to panic if things are not working out, but it is very important to move on.

The highest portion of marks for any question goes for the first line, so with each part you do sit back, think of the method to follow and then put it down.

If you do not have a clue how to do one part, leave it, come back and then **put down any sort of guess**. Marks can be gained for attempts and this is vital if you want to pass.

The two most common mistakes that you must watch out for are:

(i) not taking the question down right (minus 1 mark);
(ii) mistakes with signs (minus 3 marks).

These mistakes on their own do not cost many marks, but they may mean that the question becomes impossible to finish and that's when you lose out.

Grades

Here are the grades and the marks that you are allowed to lose out of 600 marks.

> A1 – lose 60 marks
> A2 – lose 90 marks
> B1 – lose 120 marks
> B2 – lose 150 marks
> B3 – lose 180 marks
> C1 – lose 210 marks
> C2 – lose 240 marks
> C3 – lose 270 marks
> D1 – lose 300 marks
> D2 – lose 330 marks
> D3 – lose 360 marks

Time in the exam

> 9.30 – 9.40 Read the paper.
> 9.40 – 10.00 Question 1.
> 10.00 – 10.20 Question 2.
> 10.20 – 10.40 Question 3.
> 10.40 – 11.00 Question 4.
> 11.00 – 11.20 Question 5.
> 11.20 – 11.40 Question 6.
> 11.40 – 12.00 Fill in the gaps and check answers.

Each question has three parts:

(a) part, worth 10 marks, which is very straightforward.
(b) part, worth 20 marks, which is harder.
(c) part, worth 20 marks, which is harder still.

Do not be afraid of (c) parts as they are material covered, and are generally much easier than they seem.

Marks awarded

Here in a rough way is where the marks are:

(a) parts: 3 lines that you must get to

> Line 1 = 4 marks
> Line 2 = 7 marks
> Line 3 = 10 marks
> ATTEMPT marks of 3

(b) and (c) parts: 5 lines to get to

> Line 1 = 8 marks
> Line 2 = 11 marks
> Line 3 = 14 marks
> Line 4 = 17 marks
> Line 5 = 20 marks.
> ATTEMPT marks of 6

Course content

2 papers taking 2 hours 30 minutes.

Paper 1

You must do 6 out of 8 questions. Time 20 minutes each.

Question 1: Ratio, Percentage and Tax
Question 2: Simultaneous Equations, Inequalities and Indices
Question 3: Changing Formula, Cubic Equations and Quadratic Graphs
Question 4: Complex Numbers
Question 5: Sequences and Series and Compound Interest
Question 6: Period and Range, Max–min problems and Graphs
Question 7: Differentiation
Question 8: Differentiation, Relations, Functions and Graphs.

Paper 2

You must do 5 out of 7 and 1 option out of 3. Time 20 minutes each.

Question 1: Area and volume, Simpson's Rule
Question 2: Circle
Question 3: Line
Question 4: Trigonometry
Question 5: Theorems and Enlargements
Question 6: Probability
Question 7: Statistics
Option :
Question 11: Linear Programming

There are 14 chapters in this book covering topics on the course as they appear. It is not essential to follow this order, but it is vital to cover 6 questions on both papers.

Chapter 1
Ratios, Percentage and Tax

Contents

(a) Ratio (page 1)
(b) Direct proportion (page 2)
(c) Inverse proportion (page 3)
(d) Percentages (page 4)
(e) Household bills (page 6)
(f) Distance – speed – time (page 8)
(g) Tax (page 9)
(h) Compound interest (page 10)
(i) Calculator use (page 13).

Ratio

To express one quantity as a ratio of another:

Step 1: Make sure both quantities are in the same units.

Step 2: Remove the units and write the numbers as a ratio.

Step 3: Simplify if possible.

Example: Express 30 cm as a ratio of 3 m.

Solution

Step 1: Write both in cm. 3 m = 300 cm
Step 2: 30 : 300
Step 3: 1 : 10

Example: Express 75c as a ratio of €1.50.

Solution

Write both in c.

€1.50 = 150c

75 : 150

1 : 2

To divide a number in a given ratio

Step 1: Add the ratios.

Step 2: Divide the number by this total.

Step 3: Multiply the result in step 2 by each separate ratio.

Example: Divide €360 in the ratio 4:5.

Solution

4 + 5 = 9 parts in total

9 parts = 360

1 part = $\frac{360}{9}$ = 40   can use the calculator here if need be

4 parts = 40 × 4 = 160

5 parts = 40 × 5 = 200

Example: Divide 140 m in the ratio $\frac{2}{3} : \frac{1}{2}$.

Note: Must get a common denominator between the two fractions to express the ratio as whole numbers.

Solution

$\frac{2}{3} : \frac{1}{2} = \frac{4}{6} : \frac{3}{6}$ now we can drop the common denominator

We need to divide 140 in the ratio 4:3

7 parts = 140
1 part = 20
4 parts = 80
3 parts = 60

Example: Divide €522 among A, B and C so that A gets twice B's share and C gets three times A's share.

Always take your time and try and write down a ratio in pairs first.

Solution

Ratio A : B = 2:1 since A gets twice B's share.

Ratio C : A = 3:1 since C gets three times A's share.

Now we can attempt to make a ratio using all three of A, B and C. We must try to decide who has got the least and relate everyone else to this.

A : B : C
2   1
1   3   B is bottom of the pile so he gets 1. A gets 2 (twice B) and C gets 6 (3 times A)
2   1   6

Continue as above:

9 parts = €522
1 part = €58 = B's share
2 parts = €116 = A's share
6 parts = €348 = C's share

Given the ratio and one of the answers

This time we have to let the required ratio equal a given value to form our equation.

Example: A sum of money is divided in the ratio 4:5. If the larger amount is €60, find the smaller amount.

Solution

The larger ratio is 5 and the larger amount is 60, so

5 parts = 60
1 part = 12
4 parts = 48

Example: A piece of tape is divided in the ratio of 2 : 9. If the difference between the two resultant pieces is 140 cm, find the length of the whole tape.

Solution

The difference between the ratios is 7 and the difference in lengths is 140 cm, so

7 parts = 140
1 part = 20
2 parts = 40
9 parts = 180

Length of whole tape = 40 + 180
= 220 cm

Direct proportion

As one quantity goes up, the other quantity goes up. We always try to see what the cost of ONE item is – this is called the unitary method.

Example: If a car travels 120 km on 8 litres of petrol, find:
(i) how far it will travel on 17 litres at the same rate of consumption
(ii) how many litres will be required for a journey of 280 km.

Solution

(i) 8 litres for 120 km

form a simple equation

1 litre for $\frac{120}{8}$ = 15 km

17 litres for 15 × 17 = 255 km

(ii) For every 15 km travelled we need 1 litre.

280 km needs $\frac{280}{15}$ = 18.7 litres

Foreign Exchange

Example: Find the value of $4,350 in Euros when the conversion is €1 = $1.20.

Solution

$1.20 = €1
$2.40 = €2

and if we keep going we should be able to figure out that we need to divide the amount of dollars given by 1.2.

$4,350 = $\frac{4350}{1.2}$ = €3,625

Note: The conversion rate must be stated on the paper so we do not have to know it.

Example: If €1 = $1.12, find the value of €520 in dollars.

Solution
Try as always with money to put yourself in the position of going into the bank with €520 to convert into dollars. You know that €1 = $1.12, so that for every €1 you have you get $1.12; €2 will get you $2.24 and so on. You have to multiply the number of euros you have by 1.12 to find the number of dollars.

€520 = 520 × 1.12 = $582.40

Inverse proportion

As one quantity goes up, the other quantity goes down. These questions are based in and around time.

As speed decreases, the time taken to do a job increases.

As the number of men on a job increases, the time taken decreases.

Example: It takes 12 men 15 days to build a house. How long will 20 men take to build the same house?

Solution

12 men take 15 days

1 man takes 12 × 15 days (1 man must take longer)

20 men take $\frac{180}{20}$ = 9 days

Example: When a man drinks 6 litres of water a day a container of water will last him 15 days. If he drinks only 5 litres a day, how long will the container last?

Solution

At 6 litres a day lasts 15 days

At 1 litre a day would last 6 × 15

= 90 days

At 5 litres a day would last $\frac{90}{5}$ = 18 days

Percentages

Type 1

To find a percentage of a given number

Example: Find 7% of 350.

Solution

Change 7% into a fraction by putting 7 over 100.

$$\frac{7}{100} \times \frac{350}{1} = 24.5$$

Note: To evaluate, use the calculator to multiply 7 by 350 and divide the answer by 100.

Type 2

Given a percentage and its value

Example: If 8% of a sum of money is €200, find the sum of money.

Note: The sum of money that we started with is always 100%. We need to try to form some sort of equation so that we can find 1% and then 100%.

Solution

$8\% = 200$

$1\% = \frac{200}{8} = 25$

$100\% = \frac{200}{8} \times \frac{100}{1} = 25 \times 100 = 2{,}500$

Type 3

To find one number as a percentage of another

Put the first number over the second and multiply by a hundred over one.

$$\frac{1^{st}}{2^{nd}} \times \frac{100}{1}$$

Example: Write 4.5 as a percentage of 22.5.

Solution

$$\frac{4.5}{22.5} \times \frac{100}{1} = 20\%$$

We can now use these different techniques for different questions on:
   Percentage Increase – Profit – VAT – and Discount.

Percentage increase

Example: Find a 12% increase on €800.

Solution

Find 12% of 800 and then add the answer on.

$$\frac{12}{100} \times \frac{800}{1} = \frac{9600}{100} = 96$$

Answer €800 + 96 = €896

Example: Find a 6% decrease on €150.

Solution

$$\frac{6}{100} \times \frac{150}{1} = \frac{900}{100} = 9$$

Answer 150 – 9 = €141 (decrease means value has gone down so we subtract).

Example: Ann earns €32,000 but is due an increase which will bring her salary up to €33,600. Find the percentage increase.

Solution

Increase = 33,600 − 32,000 = 1,600

$$\boxed{\text{Percentage increase} = \frac{\text{increase}}{\text{original}} \times \frac{100}{1}}$$

Percentage increase

$$= \frac{1600}{32000} \times \frac{100}{1} = 5\%$$

Example: John's salary increased by 7% to €43,500. Find his salary before the increase, to the nearest euro.

Solution

> His salary before the increase is what he started with and in terms of percentage = 100%.

His increase is what he started with plus an extra 7%, so in total is 107%.

107% = 43,500

$$1\% = \frac{43500}{107} = 406.5420$$

100% = 406.5420 × 100 = 40654.2

Answer to nearest euro = €40,654

Profit and loss

Example: A car company buys a car for €16,400. If the car makes an 8.5% profit, find its selling price.

Find 8.5% of 16,400 and add it on to the cost price.

Solution

$$\frac{8.5}{100} \times \frac{16400}{1} = 1,394$$

Answer €16,400 + 1,394 = €17,794

Example: A car costing €17,500 is sold for €19,300. Find the percentage profit to one decimal place.

Solution

We must first find the profit.

$$\boxed{\begin{array}{l}\text{Profit} = \text{sell} - \text{cost}\\ \text{Loss} = \text{cost} - \text{sell.}\end{array}}$$

Profit = 19,300 − 17,500 = 1,800

$$\boxed{\text{Percentage profit} = \frac{\text{profit}}{\text{cost}} \times \frac{100}{1}}$$

$$= \frac{1800}{17500} \times \frac{100}{1} = 10.28$$

Answer to one decimal place = 10.3%

Example: A bike is sold for €378 including a profit of 8%. Find the cost of the bike.

Solution

$$\boxed{\text{The cost price} = 100\%}$$

Profit = 8%

Selling price = 108%

We know the selling price is €378 and the percentage we sold the bike for was 108%.

108% = 378

$$1\% = \frac{378}{108} = 3.5$$

100% = 3.5 × 100 = 350

Cost price = €350

VAT

This is the tax added onto the price of a good (Value Added Tax).

Example: A bike costs €90 before VAT of 15% is added. Find the selling price of the bike.

Solution

Find 15% of 90 and add on.
Answer €103.50

Example: A bill amounts to €177.87 when VAT at 21% is included. Find the value of the VAT.

Solution

$$121\% = 177.87$$
$$1\% = \frac{177.87}{121}$$
$$100 = \frac{177.87}{121} \times \frac{21}{1} = €30.87$$

Example: A computer cost €9,560 before VAT and €10,994 with VAT included. Find the VAT rate.

Solution

$$VAT = 10{,}994 - 9{,}560 = 1{,}434$$

$$\boxed{\text{Percentage VAT} = \frac{\text{VAT}}{\text{Original}} \times \frac{100}{1}}$$

$$= \frac{1434}{9560} \times \frac{100}{1} = 15\%$$

Discounts

Example: During a sale a dishwasher is sold for €387, at a discount of 14%. Find the price of the dishwasher before the sale.

Note: Discount will reduce the value of a product.

Solution

$$\boxed{\text{Original} = 100\%}$$

Discount = 14%

Sale price = 86%

$$86\% = 387$$
$$1\% = \frac{387}{86}$$
$$100\% = \frac{387}{86} \times \frac{100}{1} = €450$$

To find a percentage error

- Add the real figures.
- Add the approximate figures.
- Subtract the two above to get the error.
- Put the error over the real and multiply by a hundred over one.

Example: Calculate the percentage error in taking 60 + 20 as an approximation for 62.21 + 24.12.

Solution

$$60 + 20 = 80 \qquad 62.21 + 24.12 = 86.33$$

$$\text{Error} = 86.33 - 80 = 6.33$$

$$\boxed{\text{Percentage error} = \frac{\text{error}}{\text{real}} \times \frac{100}{1}}$$

$$\text{Percentage error} = \frac{6.33}{86.33} \times \frac{100}{1} = 7.3\%$$

Household bills

Two of the more common types of question here use phone and electricity bills. Both of these follow the same basic format.

We need to find:

- the number of units used
- the cost of the units used; multiply units used by price per unit (which will be given)
- the standing charge (or line rental), which is a fixed charge (given in question)
- the subtotal before VAT
  = cost of units + standing charge
- the amount of VAT and add it on.

Example: The present reading on the electricity for Ann's house is 34,214 units. The previous reading was 31,562 units.

(i) How many units of electricity were used since the previous reading?
(ii) What is the cost of the electricity used, if electricity cost 7.2 cents per unit?
(iii) A standing charge of €8.50 is added and VAT is then charged on the full amount. If Ann's total bill is €214.41, calculate the rate of VAT.

Solution

(i) Units used = present − previous reading
$$= 34{,}214 - 31{,}562 = 2{,}652$$

(ii) Cost of units = units used × price
$$= 2{,}652 \times 7.2 = 19{,}094.4c$$

Note: Must convert the number of cents into euros by dividing by 100.

(iii) 19,094.4c = €190.94, to the nearest cent.

Cost of units used = €190.94
Standing charge = € 8.50
Subtotal (no VAT) = €199.44
VAT = total bill − subtotal
$$= 214.41 - 199.44 = €14.97$$

We know that we need to put 14.97 over either 199.44 or 214.41, but maybe you are not sure which one. If in doubt do both and put a line through one of them. Whichever is the right one will get you all the marks. If you do this all the time you will not get every question done; so it is better to know that we put the VAT over the subtotal (original) and multiply by 100:

$$\text{Answer} = \frac{14.97}{199.44} \times \frac{100}{1} = 7.5\%$$

There are many other practical problems that can be asked. Follow what is asked in the question and try to figure it out using common sense.

Example: A raffle to raise money for a charity is being held.

The first prize is €100, the second is €85, the third is €65 and the fourth is €50.

The cost of printing tickets is €42 for the first 500 tickets and €6 for each additional 100 tickets. The smallest number of tickets that can be printed is 500.

Tickets are being sold at €1.50 each.

(i) What is the minimum possible cost of the raffle?
(ii) If 500 tickets are printed, how many tickets must be sold in order to avoid a loss?
(iii) If 1,000 tickets are printed and 65% of the tickets are sold, how much money will be raised for the charity?

Solution

(i) The minimum cost will be the cost of the 500 tickets and the total prize money that must be given out.

$$€42 + €100 + €85 + €65 + €50$$
$$= €342$$

7

(ii) In order to avoid a loss we need to get at least €342 in total at €1.50 per ticket.
To find number of tickets divide 342 by 1.5 = 228 tickets.

(iii) We need to figure out the total cost and the total money received.

When there are 1,000 tickets printed that means we not only have to pay €342 for the first 500 tickets and the prize fund, but we also need to pay for an extra 500 tickets at €6 per 100 tickets.

Extra 500 tickets will cost 5 × 6 = €30

Total cost = €342 + €30 = €372

To find total money received we need to multiply the number of tickets sold by €1.50.

65% of the 1,000 tickets were sold = 650 tickets at €1.50 = total received of €975.

Money raised = €975 − €372
= €603

Distance – speed – time

This comes down to two types of question.
Type 1. Questions where we must make use of 'Dad's silly triangle'.
Type 2. To convert from m/s to km/h, or vice versa.

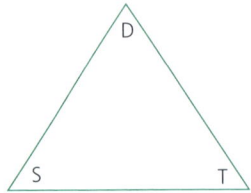

Distance = Speed × Time,

Speed = $\frac{\text{Distance}}{\text{Time}}$, Time = $\frac{\text{Distance}}{\text{Speed}}$

Example: A cyclist started a journey of 56 km at 1015 and finished the journey at 1135 hours. Calculate the average speed of the cyclist in km/h.

When we deal with time we always change it to hours unless told to use minutes.

Solution

1135 − 1015 = 1 hour 20 minutes

20 minutes = $\frac{1}{3}$ of an hour

Speed = $\frac{\text{Distance}}{\text{Time}}$

= $\frac{56}{1\frac{1}{3}}$

= 42 km/h

Use the calculator. Put in 56, divide by 1 [abc] 1 [abc] 3

Note: [abc] is the fraction button on the calculator.

Need to know 2 conversions:
1 km = 1,000 m
1 hour = 3,600 seconds.

Example: Convert 3 m/s into km/h.

Solution

1 hour = 3,600 seconds, so to convert from seconds to hours multiply by 3,600

3 m/s = 10,800 m/h

1,000 m = 1 km, so to convert from metres to kilometres divide by 1,000

3 m/s = 10,800 m/h = 10.8 km/h.

Tax

- We are taxed at a certain rate on the gross income.
- Find percentage of gross income = gross tax.
- Gross tax – tax credits = net tax (tax we actually pay).
- Take-home pay = gross income – net tax.

Type 1

When there is only one tax rate

Example: John earns €50,000. He pays tax at a rate of 22% of his gross income. If he has tax credits of €7,500, find his take-home pay.

Solution

Gross tax = 22% of €50,000

$$= \frac{22}{100} \times \frac{50000}{1} = €11,000$$

Net tax = 11,000 – 7,500 = €3,500

Take-home pay = 50,000 – 3,500
$$= €46,500$$

Type 2

When there are two tax rates

Example: Tom earns €33,500 a year. He has tax credits of €7,400. If he pays tax at a rate of 22% at lower rate and 40% at higher rate, find his net income if he has a standard rate cut-off point of €21,000.

Solution

His tax payments are split into two parts.
 €21,000 at lower rate
 €12,500 at higher rate
 (33,500 – 21,000)

Find 22% of €21,000 = €4,620
Find 40% of €12,500 = €5,000
 Gross tax = €9,620

 Gross tax = €9,620
 Tax credits = €7,400
 Tax paid = €2,220

Take-home pay = €33,500 – €2,220
 = €31,280

Type 3

To find the gross wage

Example: John pays €7,850 in tax for the year. He has tax credits of €4,600 and a standard rate cut-off point of €21,000. The standard rate of tax is 22% and the higher rate is 40% on all income above the standard rate cut-off point. Calculate John's gross income for the year.

Solution

We must find the gross tax for John.
Net tax = €7,850

Gross tax = net tax + tax credits
 = €7,850 + €4,600 = €12,450

His gross tax bill is €12,450, which is made up of standard rate tax and higher rate tax.

 Standard rate tax = 22% of €21,000
 = €4,620

His total tax is €12,450 of which €4,620

9

is paid at the lower rate, so the rest (€12,450 – €4,620 = €7,830) must be what he has paid at the higher rate.

Higher rate = 40%. Amount due at higher tax rate = €7,830, so to figure out how much money he had at higher rate let 40% = €7,830 and find the original amount (i.e. 100%)

$$40\% = 7{,}830$$
$$1\% = \frac{7830}{40} = 195.75$$
$$100\% = 195.75 \times 100 = €19{,}575$$

Gross wage = lower tax band
+ higher tax band
= €21,000 + €19,575
= €40,575

Compound interest

Principal = the amount of money put into the bank.

Interest = the money made on my principal.

Time = the length of time in years that the principal is in the bank.

Rate = the rate of interest (a percentage of the principal).

In the case of *simple interest* we just follow the formula:

$$I = \frac{PTR}{100}$$

The important point about *compound interest* is that at the end of the year interest is added to the principal.
$$A = P + I.$$

The amount at the end of the year 1 becomes the principal at the start of year 2.

Example: €9,000 is invested for 2 years compound interest. The rate of interest in the first year is 5%, the second year 6.5%. Calculate the total interest earned.

Solution

Make sure to split the question up so that you answer it year by year.

Year 1: P_1 = 9,000, R = 5

$$\boxed{\text{Interest} = \frac{PR}{100}} = \frac{9000 \times 5}{100} = 450$$

A_1 = 9,000 + 450 = 9,450

Year 2: P_2 = 9,450, R = 6.5

$$\text{Interest} = \frac{PR}{100} = \frac{9450 \times 6.5}{100} = 614.25$$

Total interest = interest in year 1
+ interest in year 2
= 450 + 614.25
= €1,064.25

Example: €4,500 is borrowed for 2 years at 8% per annum. If €1,200 is paid back at the end of the first year, how much is owed at the end of the second year?

Same methods as above except we have to subtract the repayment at the end of year 1.

Solution

Year 1: P_1 = 4,500, R = 8

$$\text{Interest} = \frac{PR}{100}$$
$$= \frac{4500 \times 8}{100} = 360$$

A_1 = 4,500 + 360 = €4,860

At the end of the year €1,200 is paid back, so the principal for year 2 will be 4,860 − 1,200 = €3,660.

Year 2: $P_2 = 3,660$, $R = 8$

$$\text{Interest} = \frac{PR}{100} = \frac{3660 \times 8}{100} = 292.80$$

$A_2 = 3,660 + 292.80 = €3,952.80$

Note: Per annum means per year.

Example: A sum of money invested at compound interest amounts to €1,984.50 after two years at 5% per annum. Calculate the sum invested.

In this question we have what we ended year 2 with, so we must start at year 2 and work backwards.

In terms of percentages we started the year with 100% and in this question we gained 5%, so that at the end of the year we had 105% of what we started the year with. Therefore at the end of year 2 we have 105% of what we started the year with.

Solution

Year 2:   105% = 1,984.50

　　　　　 1% = 18.9

　　　　　 100% = 1,890

Now we repeat the same process for year 1.

Year 1:   105% = 1,890

　　　　　 1% = 18

　　　　　 100% = 1,800

The original amount was €1,800.

Example: A sum of money, €40,000, is invested for 3 years at compound interest. The rate of interest for year 1 is 10% and for year 2 is also 10%. Calculate how much the invested money amounts to at the end of year 2.

At the end of year 3, the invested money amounted to €51,667. Calculate the rate of interest for year 3.

Solution

Year 1: $P_1 = 40,000$, $R = 10$

$$\text{Interest} = \frac{PR}{100} = \frac{40000 \times 10}{100} = 4,000$$

$A_1 = 40,000 + 4,000 = €44,000$

Year 2: $P_2 = 44,000$, $R = 10$

$$\text{Interest} = \frac{PR}{100} = \frac{44000 \times 10}{100} = 4,400$$

$A_2 = 44,000 + 4,400 = €48,400$

Year 3: $P_3 = 48,400$, $A_3 = 51,667$

$$\boxed{\text{Interest} = \text{amount} - \text{principal}}$$

$= 51,667 - 48,400 = €3,267$

$$\text{Percentage interest} = \frac{\text{interest}}{\text{principal}} \times \frac{100}{1}$$

$$= \frac{3267}{48400} \times \frac{100}{1} = 6.75\%$$

Example: How much money must be invested for 2 years with compound interest at 8% per annum in order to earn €777.60 in interest in the second year?

Solution

When the principal is unknown, as in this question, let the principal be €100 and continue.

Year 1: $P_1 = 100$, $R = 8$

$$\text{Interest} = \frac{PR}{100} = \frac{100 \times 8}{100} = 8$$

$A_1 = 108$

11

Year 2: $P_2 = 108$, $R = 8$

Interest = $\dfrac{PR}{100} = \dfrac{108 \times 8}{100} = 8.64$

This means that for every €100 invested we gain €8.64 in interest in the second year.

The number of €100 that we must invest is therefore given by $\dfrac{777.7}{8.64} = 90$.

The amount we must invest is €9,000.

Example: A sum of money, €5,900, is invested for one year. The rate of interest is 8%. Calculate how much the invested money amounts to at the end of year 1.

A charge of €x was then deducted from this amount. The money which remained was converted into dollars and the dollars were invested for a year at a rate of interest of 9% per annum.

At the end of the year, the invested dollars amounted to $10,137. If the exchange was €1 = $1.50 on the day the euros were changed into dollars, calculate x.

Solution

Year 1: $P_1 = 5,900$, $R = 8$

Interest = $\dfrac{PR}{100} = \dfrac{5900 \times 8}{100} = 472$

$A_1 = $ €6,372

Year 2: Need to work backwards since we have the amount.

$$109\% = 10,137$$
$$1\% = 93$$
$$100\% = \$9,300$$

Now convert the dollars to euros:

$\dfrac{9300}{1.5} = $ €6,200

$x = 6,372 - 6,200 = $ €172

Compound interest formula

To find what a principal (P) amounts to (A) after a number of years (n) at the same rate of interest (r), use the formula

$$A = P\left(1 + \dfrac{r}{100}\right)^n$$

Example: Find what €6,000 amounts to after 4 years at 6% per annum.

Solution

$P = 6000$, $r = 6$, $n = 4$; find A.

$A = P\left(1 + \dfrac{r}{100}\right)^n$

$= 6,000\left(1 + \dfrac{6}{100}\right)^4$ put the figures in

$= 6,000(1 + 0.06)^4$ change fraction to decimal and add

$= 6,000(1.06)^4$

powers first then multiply

$= 6,000 (1.262476)$

$= 7,574.856$

Answer €7,574.86 to one decimal place.

Example: At what rate will €5,000 amount to €6,655 after 3 years, at the same compound interest each year?

Solution

$P = 5,000$, $A = 6,655$, $n = 3$; find r.

$A = P\left(1 + \dfrac{r}{100}\right)^n$

put the figures in

$6,655 = 5,000\left(1 + \dfrac{r}{100}\right)^3$

change fraction to decimal and add

$$6{,}655 = 5{,}000(1 + 0.01r)^3$$

divide by 5,000

$$\frac{6655}{5000} = (1 + 0.01r)^3$$

$$(1 + 0.01r)^3 = 1.331$$

cube root both sides

$$1 + 0.01r = 1.1$$

$$0.01r = 0.1$$

multiply both sides by 100

$$r = 10$$

Calculator use

Decimal places

This applies when we are asked to round off our answer to a required number of decimal places.

If we are asked to round off to two decimal places, we need to have only two digits after the decimal point.

Example: Round 3.567 off to two decimal places

Solution

Go to the third digit; if it is four or less, leave the digit in front alone. If it is 5 or more, round the digit in front up by one.

$$3.567 = 3.57$$

Example: Round 23.6953
 (i) to one decimal place
 (ii) to two decimal places
 (iii) to three decimal places.

Solution

(i) One decimal place – look at the second digit after the decimal.

$$23.6953 = 23.7$$

(ii) Two decimal places – look at the third digit after the decimal.

$$23.6953 = 23.7,$$ since when we round up 69 becomes 70

(iii) Three decimal places – look at the fourth digit after the decimal.

$$23.6953 = 23.695$$

Square roots

$$\sqrt{41.5} = 41.5 \boxed{\sqrt{}} = 6.44$$

Powers

$$(4.1)^3 = 4.1 \boxed{y^x} \, 3 = 68.921$$

Fractions

$$\frac{1}{3.5} = 1 \boxed{\div} \, 3.5 = 0.2875714286$$

How to work with fractions on the calculator

We need to be able to use the $\boxed{a^b/c}$ key.

Example: Find the value of:

(i) $\frac{1}{2} + \frac{1}{3}$

(ii) $1\frac{2}{3} + 2\frac{3}{5}$

(iii) $3\frac{1}{2} \times 4\frac{3}{5}$

Solution

(i) $\frac{1}{2} + \frac{1}{3}$

$1 \boxed{a^b/c} 2 + 1 \boxed{a^b/c} 3 = \frac{5}{6}$

Note: When you use the calculator $1 \boxed{a^b/c} 2$ appears as $1 \text{ r } 2\frac{1}{2}$.

(ii) $1\frac{2}{3} + 2\frac{3}{5}$

$1 \boxed{a^b/c} 2 \boxed{a^b/c} 3 + 2 \boxed{a^b/c} 3 \boxed{a^b/c} 5$

$= 4 \text{ r } 4 \text{ r } 15 = 4\frac{4}{15}$

(iii) $3\frac{1}{2} \times 4\frac{3}{5}$

$3 \boxed{a^b/c} 1 \boxed{a^b/c} 2 \times 4 \boxed{a^b/c} 3 \boxed{a^b/c} 5$

$= 16 \text{ r } 1 \text{ r } 10 = 16\frac{1}{10}$

Scientific notation

This is one of the easier parts to deal with, as we use the $\boxed{\text{EXP}}$ button on the calculator.

A number in scientific notation is written in the form $a.bc \times 10^n$, i.e. it has only one digit before the decimal point.

A big number has a positive power on the 10.

$2,300,000 = 2.3 \times 10^6$

$1.5 \times 10^4 = 15,000$

A small number has a negative power on the 10.

$0.0000023 = 2.3 \times 10^{-6}$

$1.5 \times 10^{-4} = 0.00015$

Example: Find the value of $2.5 \times 10^{-5} + 1.4 \times 10^{-6}$ in the form $a.bc \times 10^n$.

Solution

$2.5 \times 10^{-5} + 1.4 \times 10^{-6}$

All of this is done on the calculator as follows:

$2.5 \boxed{\text{EXP}} 5 \boxed{\pm} + 1.4 \boxed{\text{EXP}} 6 \boxed{\pm}$

$= 0.0000264$

$= 2.64 \times 10^{-5}$

Note: We must change 0.0000264 back into scientific notation, so we need to move the decimal to after the first digit. Count the number of places the decimal has moved. Remember that small numbers have a negative power on the 10.

Example: Find the value of each of the following:

(i) $(3.4 \times 10^5) \times (2.1 \times 10^6)$

(ii) $(2.5 \times 10^3)^2$

(iii) $\dfrac{3.6 \times 10^4}{1.2 \times 10^2}$

(iv) $\dfrac{(2.1 \times 10^3) \times (4 \times 10^5)}{7 \times 10^{-2}}$

Solution

(i) 3.4 $\boxed{\text{EXP}}$ 5×2.1 $\boxed{\text{EXP}}$ 6

$= 7.14 \times 10^{11}$

(ii) $(2.5 \times 10^3)^2$ squared means multiply by itself

$= (2.5 \times 10^3) \times (2.5 \times 10^3)$

$= 2.5$ $\boxed{\text{EXP}}$ 3×2.5 $\boxed{\text{EXP}}$ 3

$= 6{,}250{,}000$

$= 6.25 \times 10^6$

Note: We must change 6,250,000 back into scientific notation, so we need to move the decimal to after the first digit. Count the number of places the decimal has moved. Remember that big numbers have a positive power on the 10.

(iii) 3.6 $\boxed{\text{EXP}}$ $4 \div 1.2$ $\boxed{\text{EXP}}$ 2

$= 300$

$= 3 \times 10^2$

(iv) $(2.1 \times 10^3) \times (4 \times 10^5)$

$= 2.1$ $\boxed{\text{EXP}}$ 3×4 $\boxed{\text{EXP}}$ 5

$= 8{,}400{,}000{,}000$

$8{,}400{,}000{,}000 \div 7$ $\boxed{\text{EXP}}$ 2 $\boxed{\pm}$

$= 1.2 \times 10^{11}$

Note: In the last example, split it up. Do out the top first and then divide by the bottom.

Chapter 2
Algebra

Contents

(a) To add and subtract (page 16)
(b) To multiply (page 16)
(c) Evaluating expressions (page 17)
(d) To solve equations (page 18)
(e) Factorisation (page 19)
(f) To add and subtract fractions (page 23)
(g) Manipulation of formulae (page 24)
(h) Inequalities (page 25)
(i) Quadratic equations (page 26)
(j) To solve simultaneous equations (page 30)
(k) Cubic equations (page 32)
(l) Indices (page 33).

To add and subtract

Only add like to like – add the numbers in front only, not the powers.

Note: Like terms contain the same letters and have the same powers.

Example:

(i) $2a + 3b - 6a + 3b$

$\quad = -4a + 6b$

(ii) $2x^2 + 3x - 2x + 7$

$\quad = 2x^2 + x + 7$

To multiply

When multiplying letters that are the same, add the powers.

Example: Simplify

$$x^2 \cdot x^3 = x^5$$

Multiply the number in front and then add the powers on the same letters.

Note: If there is no number in front, then it is 1.

Example: Simplify

$$(2x)(3x) = 6x^2$$

$$3ab^2(5a^2b^2) = 15a^3b^4$$

Dealing with brackets

Step 1: Multiply everything inside the brackets by what is outside.
Step 2: Add and subtract like terms.

Example: Simplify each of the following:

(i) $2a(b + c) - 3b(a + 2c)$

$\quad = 2ab + 2ac - 3ab - 6bc$

$\quad = -ab + 2ac - 6bc$

(ii) $x(x - 1) - 3(x - 1)$

$\quad = x^2 - x - 3x + 3$

$\quad = x^2 - 4x + 3$

Double brackets

Split the first up into two and put the second down twice.

Example: Simplify each of the following products.

$\quad (x + 3)(x - 2)$

Solution

split the first bracket and write second one down twice

$\quad = x(x - 2) + 3(x - 2)$

multiply what's outside by what's inside

$\quad = x^2 - 2x + 3x - 6$

add or subtract like terms

$\quad = x^2 + x - 6$

Note: Square means multiply by itself.

Example: Simplify $(2x - 3)^2$

Solution

$(2x - 3)^2 = (2x - 3)(2x - 3)$

square means multiply by itself

$\quad = 2x(2x - 3) - 3(2x - 3)$

split the first one up

$\quad = 4x^2 - 6x - 6x + 9$

$\quad = 4x^2 - 12x + 9$

Evaluating expressions

Put number in instead of the letters.

Here we can use the calculator to obtain our answer. You must practise with your calculator, as each one is slightly different.

Remember when using a calculator:

(i) Do not be greedy – do not do it all at once until you have a line with no squares or fractions.
(ii) Square first, then multiply.
(iii) Write down results as you go along.

Example: If $a = 3$ and $b = -4$ find the value of each of the following:

(i) $\quad 2a + 4b$

put the numbers in for the letters

$\quad = 2(3) + 4(-4) = -10$

Once we have a line with only addition and multiplication, then the calculator will do the rest.

On the calculator put in

$\quad 2 \times 3 + 4 \times 4 \pm = -10$

(watch for the signs)

(ii) $\quad 2a^2 - b^2$

$\quad = 2(3)^2 - (-4)^2 \quad$ square first

$\quad = 2(9) - 16$

$\quad = 2 \times 9 - 16$

$\quad = 2$

17

To solve equations

Bring required letter to one side, numbers to the other.
Always get rid of division first by finding a common denominator.
When a term crosses the equals sign, it changes sign.
To get rid of multiplication – divide.

Example: Solve for x:
$$2x + 1 = 9$$
Solution
$$2x = 9 - 1$$
when a number crosses the equals sign it changes sign
$$2x = 8$$
to get rid of multiplication divide
$$x = \frac{8}{2}$$
$$x = 4$$

Note: In reality the question above is done quickly by not showing each step.
$$2x + 1 = 9$$
add becomes subtract
$$2x = 8$$
multiply becomes divide
$$x = 4$$

Example: Solve: $5x + 1 = 2x - 5$.
Solution
$$5x + 1 = 2x - 5$$
letters to left, numbers to right; when a term crosses the equals it changes sign

$$3x = -6$$
multiply becomes divide
$$x = -2$$

Example: Solve: $4(x - 1) = 2(x + 5)$.
Solution
$$4(x - 1) = 2(x + 5)$$
multiply out: letters to left, numbers to right
$$4x - 4 = 2x + 10$$
subtract becomes add and add becomes subtract
$$2x = 14$$
multiply becomes divide
$$x = 7$$

Example: Solve: $\frac{2x - 1}{3} = 4$.

put the 4 over 1 and get a common denominator
$$\frac{2x - 1}{3} = \frac{4}{1}$$
find the common denominator of 3
$$\frac{2x - 1}{3} = \frac{4(3)}{3}$$
drop the bottom
$$2x - 1 = 12$$
letters to left, numbers to right
$$2x = 13$$
multiply becomes divide
$$x = \frac{13}{2}$$
(the answer does not have to be a whole number)

Example: Solve: $\dfrac{3x-2}{3} = \dfrac{x+1}{2}$.

Solution

common denominator of 6

$$\dfrac{2(3x-2) = 3(x+1)}{6}$$

drop the common denominator

$$2(3x-2) = 3(x+1)$$
$$6x - 4 = 3x + 3$$
$$3x = 7$$
$$x = \dfrac{7}{3}$$

Example: Solve: $\dfrac{3x-5}{x-2} = 2$.

Solution

Put the 2 over 1 and get a common denominator

$$\dfrac{3x-5}{x-2} = \dfrac{2}{1}$$
$$\dfrac{3x-5 = 2(x-2)}{x-2}$$
$$3x - 5 = 2x - 4$$
$$x = 1$$

Factorisation

Type 1

Factors by Grouping – 2 or 4 terms – take out what's common.

Example: Factorise each of the following (very important):

(i) $3x - 4x^2$
(ii) $2a^2b - 4ab^2$

Solution

(i) $3x - 4x^2$ take out the x

   $= x(3 - 4x)$

(ii) $2a^2b - 4ab^2$

take out the common $2ab$

   $= 2ab(a - 2b)$

In the above we had only two terms, but if we have four terms we group them in twos according to the letters.

We therefore recognise these questions because they have either two or four terms.

Example: Factorise each of the following (not asked often):

(i) $2ac - 3bd - bc + 6ad$
(ii) $ab + a - b - 1$

Solution

Since there are four terms in the questions we know it is factorisation by grouping, so we try to group like terms.

(i) $2ac - 3bd - bc + 6ad$

nothing common so swap terms around

   $= 2ac - bc + 6ad - 3bd$

in the first two take out c, from next two terms take out $3d$

   $= c(2a - b) + 3d(2a - b)$

take out what's common $(2a - b)$

   $= (2a - b)(c + 3d)$

(ii) $ab + a - b - 1$

   $= a(b + 1) - 1(b + 1)$
   $= (a - 1)(b + 1)$

Note: In the last example watch out for two things:

19

(a) Must have the same expression in both brackets, so took out –1.
(b) If nothing will go into two terms we can always take out 1.

Type 2

> Quadratic Factors (very, very important section)

There are two very different types of quadratic equation, but the rules for dealing with each change only slightly. There are also two methods to do these questions, one of which is longer but more foolproof than the other:

(a) guide number (longer method)
(b) double brackets (quicker but can be harder to see).

A quadratic equation has x to the power of two. It is of the form $ax^2 + bx + c$.

Guide Number

To get the guide number, multiply the number in front of the x^2 by the last number (constant).

Type 1

> Quadratic where the second sign is +
>
> Want two numbers multiplied to give the guide number, but *added* to give the coefficient of x (number in front of the x).

Example: Factorise each of the following:

(i) $x^2 + 7x + 12$
(ii) $x^2 - 6x + 8$

Solution

(i) Coefficient of x^2 is 1, by the constant, which is 12 so guide number of 12.

We want two numbers to multiply to +12 and add to 7. Ans 3 and 4.

$x^2 + 7x + 12$
$= x^2 + 3x + 4x + 12$
$= x(x + 3) + 4(x + 3)$
$= (x + 4)(x + 3)$

(ii) Coefficient of x^2 is 1, by the constant, which is 8 so guide number of 8.

We want two numbers to multiply to + 8 and add to –6. Ans –2 and –4.

$x^2 - 6x + 8$
$= x^2 - 2x - 4x + 8$
$= x(x - 2) - 4(x - 2)$
$= (x - 2)(x - 4)$

Type 2

> Quadratic where the second sign is –
>
> Want two numbers multiplied to give the guide number, but *subtracted* to give the coefficient of x (number in front of the x).

Example: Factorise each of the following:

(i) $x^2 + 5x - 14$
(ii) $x^2 - 5x - 24$

Solution

(i) Coefficient of x^2 is 1, by the constant, which is –14 so guide number of –14.

We want two numbers to multiply to –14 and subtract to +5. Ans +7 and –2.

$x^2 + 5x - 14$

$= x^2 + 7x - 2x - 14$

$= x(x + 7) - 2(x + 7)$

$= (x + 7)(x - 2)$

(ii) Coefficient of x^2 is 1, by the constant, which is –24 so guide number of –24.

We want two numbers to multiply to –24 and subtract to –5. Ans –8 and +3.

$x^2 - 5x - 24$

$= x^2 - 8x + 3x - 24$

$= x(x - 8) + 3(x - 8)$

$= (x + 3)(x - 8)$

Note: When there is a number in front of the x^2 we follow the same rules as above, but we must be more careful when finding the guide number.

Example: Factorise:

(i) $2x^2 - 13x + 18$
(ii) $3x^2 - x - 14$

Solution

(i) Coefficient of x^2 is 2, by the constant, which is +18 so guide number of +36.

We want two numbers to multiply to + 36 and add to –13. Ans –4 and –9.

$2x^2 - 13x + 18$

$= 2x^2 - 4x - 9x + 18$

$= 2x(x - 2) - 9(x - 2)$

$= (2x - 9)(x - 2)$

(ii) Coefficient of x^2 is 3, by the constant, which is –14 so guide number of –42.

We want two numbers to multiply to –42 and subtract to –1. Ans –7 and +6.

$3x^2 - x - 14$

$= 3x^2 - 7x + 6x - 14$

$= x(3x - 7) + 2(3x - 7)$

$= (x + 2)(3x - 7)$

Double brackets

Type 1

Quadratic where the second sign is +

Want two numbers multiplied to give the constant, but *added* to give the middle.

Example: Factorise:

(i) $x^2 + 6x + 8$
(ii) $x^2 - 7x + 12$

These are done by trial and error, so that if we do not get the right answer the first time we have to go again. A lot of students will not write down what they are thinking and try to do the questions in their head, which for harder questions ends up taking longer. Write down what you are thinking; if it is not right put a line through it and try again.

Solution

(i) $x^2 + 6x + 8$

We put down two empty brackets.
We must split up the x^2 into each bracket as x and x. We must also split the 8 into its factors 1 by 8 or 2 by 4. In order to see which is the right answer we multiply the two inside parts and the two

21

outside parts and add the answers in the hope of obtaining the value of the middle term of our question.

$(x + 1)(x + 8)$ $x + 8x = 9x$
                    no good so try again
$(x + 2)(x + 4)$ $2x + 4x = 6x$
                    right answer

(ii) $x^2 - 7x + 12$
$(x - 1)(x - 12)$ $-x - 12x = -13x$
                    no good
$(x - 2)(x - 6)$ $-2x - 6x = -8x$
                    no good
$(x - 3)(x - 4)$ $-3x - 4x = -7x$
                    right answer

Type 2

Quadratic where the second sign is −
Want two numbers multiplied to give the constant, but *subtract* to give the middle.

Example: Factorise:

(i) $x^2 - 2x - 8$
(ii) $x^2 + 5x - 6$

Solution

(i) $x^2 - 2x - 8$
$(x + 4)(x - 2)$ $4x - 2x = 2x$

right figures but wrong signs, so change the signs

$(x - 4)(x + 2)$

(ii) $x^2 + 5x - 6$
$(x + 6)(x - 1)$ $6x - x = 5x$

When there is a number in front of the x^2 we follow the same rules as above, but it may take a little longer.

Example: Factorise:

(i) $2x^2 - 7x + 6$
(ii) $3x^2 - 2x - 8$

We must split up the $2x^2$ into each bracket as $2x$ and x. We must also split the 6 into its factors 2 by 3 or 1 by 6. I would always start with the smaller factors of 2 by 3 and remember to switch them around into 3 by 2 either.

Solution

(i) $2x^2 - 7x + 6$
$(2x - 2)(x - 3)$ $-2x - 6x = -8x$
                    no good
$(2x - 3)(x - 2)$ $-3x - 4x = -7x$ right

(ii) $3x^2 - 2x - 8$
$(3x - 2)(x + 4)$ $-2x + 12x = 10x$
                    no good
$(3x - 4)(x + 2)$ $-4x + 6x = 2x$
                    wrong sign
$(3x + 4)(x - 2)$ $4x - 6x = -2x$ right

Type 3

Difference of two squares (important section)

If we have two terms both squared with a minus in the middle we can use the following formula:

$$x^2 - y^2 = (x - y)(x + y)$$

This can be rewritten as

$$(1st)^2 - (2nd)^2 = (1st + 2nd)(1st - 2nd)$$

Example: Factorise each of the following:

(i) $a^2 - 36$
(ii) $4x^2 - 25$

Solution

(i) $a^2 - 6^2$

write both as squares and use formula
$$= (a - 6)(a + 6)$$

(ii) $(2x)^2 - 5^2$
$$= (2x - 5)(2x + 5)$$

There are two harder types of question, which include factorisation by grouping as well as the difference of two squares.

Example: Factorise:

(i) $2x^3 - 50x$
(ii) $3x^2 - 12$

Solution

(i) $2x(x^2 - 25)$

take out what's common

$2x(x - 5)(x + 5)$

difference of two squares

(ii) $3x^2 - 12$

take out the 3 that is common

$3(x^2 - 4)$

$3(x - 2)(x + 2)$

To add and subtract fractions

Step 1: Find a common denominator by multiplying the bottom expressions.
Step 2: Change the top as shown below.
Step 3: Tidy the top if possible.

Example: Write as a single fraction:

$$\frac{2}{2x + 1} - \frac{5}{3x + 2}$$

Solution

$$\frac{2}{2x + 1} - \frac{5}{3x + 2}$$

common denominator is $(2x + 1)(3x + 2)$

$$= \frac{2(3x + 2) - 5(2x + 1)}{(2x + 1)(3x + 2)}$$

note below

$$= \frac{6x + 4 - 10x - 5}{(2x + 1)(3x + 2)}$$

multiply out and then add and subtract on top line

$$= \frac{-4x - 1}{(2x + 1)(3x + 2)}$$

Note: We started the first fraction with $2x + 1$ on the bottom, which has now changed into $(2x + 1)(3x + 2)$. Since we have multiplied the bottom by $(3x + 2)$, we must also multiply the top by $(3x + 2)$. For the second fraction we multiplied the bottom by $(2x + 1)$, so multiply the top by $(2x + 1)$ as well.

Example: Write as a single fraction:

$$\frac{3}{2x - 1} - 6$$

Note: When there is a whole number put it over 1 and then get the common denominator.

Solution

$$\frac{3}{2x - 1} - \frac{6}{1}$$

common denominator $2x - 1$

$$\frac{3(1) - 6(2x - 1)}{2x - 1}$$

$$\frac{3 - 12x + 6}{2x - 1}$$

$$\frac{9 - 12x}{2x - 1}$$

23

Manipulation of formulae

This can be done if you try to follow the rules laid out below.

We will always be told to have one letter on one side and therefore we must have all the other letters on the other side.

The order in which we get rid of letters and numbers is important and we will always follow the rules:

(a) Get rid of square root by squaring both sides.
(b) Get rid of any division by multiplying *every term* by the common denominator.
(c) Get rid of addition or subtraction remembering that when we cross the equals sign we change sign.
(d) Get rid of multiplication by dividing the other side.
(e) Get rid of square by finding the square root of the other side.

> All of these come down to a simple idea, which is: to get rid of an operation, do the opposite operation.

Example: Express each of the following in terms of x:

(i) $ax + b = c$
(ii) $a(x + b) = c$
(iii) $\dfrac{a + b}{x} = c$
(iv) $ax + b = x + c$
(v) $a + \dfrac{b}{x} = c$

Every term with x to one side and every other term to other side.

Solution

(i) $ax + b = c$

add becomes subtract
$$ax = c - b$$
multiply becomes divide
$$x = \frac{c - b}{a}$$

(ii) $a(x + b) = c$

multiply out brackets
$$ax + ab = c$$
add becomes subtract
$$ax = c - ab$$
multiply becomes divide
$$x = \frac{c - ab}{a}$$

(iii) $\dfrac{a + b}{x} = c$

divide becomes multiply
$$a + b = cx$$
swap both sides
$$cx = a + b$$
multiply becomes divide
$$x = \frac{a + b}{c}$$

(iv) $ax + b = x + c$

x terms to one side
$$ax - x = c - b$$
take out the common x by factorising by grouping
$$x(a - 1) = c - b$$
$$x = \frac{c - b}{a - 1}$$

Here we have the idea that when there is more than one term with x we bring all the terms with x to one side, and then factorise by taking out the common x.

(v) $\quad a + \dfrac{b}{x} = c$

multiply each term by the common denominator

$$ax + b = cx$$
$$ax - cx = -b$$
$$x(a - c) = -b$$
$$x = \dfrac{-b}{a - c}$$

Inequalities

We deal with inequalities in the same way as equalities.
When we multiply or divide by a minus, the inequality sign must change sign (all or nothing).

We must be able to draw a number line for the different types of number set.
Natural numbers (N) – positive whole numbers
Integers (Z) – positive and negative whole numbers
Real numbers (R) – any number including fractions and decimals.

Example: Solve the inequality
$1 - 2x \geq -5$ for $x \in N$
and show on a number line.

Solution

$\quad -2x \geq -6 \quad$ letters to left, numbers to right, watch signs

$\quad 2x \leq 6 \quad$ change sign then change inequality

$\quad x \leq 3 \quad$ divide across by 2

Ans $\quad x = \{0, 1, 2, 3\}$

Note: Since the question says $x \in N$ we are allowed only whole, positive results

Example: Solve the inequality
$3x - 1 \leq 2x - 5$ for $x \in R$
and illustrate the solutions on a number line.

Solution

$$3x - 1 \leq 2x - 5$$
$$3x - 2x \leq -5 + 1$$

letters to left, numbers to the right

$$x \leq -4$$

Double inequalities

When there are two inequality signs in the question, split the question into two.

Example: Solve $5 + x < 3x - 1 < 11 + 2x$.

Solution

Left to middle

$$5 + x < 3x - 1$$
$$-2x < -6$$
$$x > 3$$

Middle to right

$$3x - 1 < 11 + 2x$$
$$x < 12$$

Answer

$$3 < x < 12$$

25

Quadratic equations

If we are asked to solve a quadratic equation we:

(a) Bring all three terms to the left-hand side and put equal to zero.
(b) Factorise the quadratic to find the two factors.
(c) Let each factor equal zero and solve to find the two roots.

Note 1: A quadratic has 2 or 3 terms, one of which has an x^2.

Note 2: Factors are the double brackets which when multiplied out give us the quadratic

e.g. $(x + 3)(x + 4) = x^2 + 7x + 12$

Note 3: Roots are the points on the quadratic where the quadratic cuts the x-axis.

Example: Solve each of the following equations:

(i) $x^2 - 4x - 32 = 0$
(ii) $x^2 + 9x = 10$

Note: To solve a quadratic equation we must first find the factors, using guide number or double brackets, if there are 3 terms. If there are 2 terms, we factorise using grouping or the difference between two squares.

Solution

(i) Guide number of -32, need two numbers to multiply to 32 and subtract to -4

$$x^2 - 4x - 32 = 0$$
$$x^2 - 8x + 4x - 32 = 0$$
$$x(x - 8) + 4(x - 8) = 0$$
$$(x + 4)(x - 8) = 0$$

Let each factor = 0 and solve the equation

$x + 4 = 0$ or $x - 8 = 0$
$x = -4$ or $x = 8$

Note: Really important that when you see an equals sign and a square in the question, you realise that it is a quadratic equation and that you must bring all the terms to the left-hand side and let the whole equation equal 0, before you start to factorise.

(ii) $\quad x^2 + 9x = 10$

bring the 10 to left and let equation = 0

$$x^2 + 9x - 10 = 0$$

guide number -10, so multiply to -10, subtract to 9

$$x^2 + 10x - x - 10 = 0$$
$$x(x + 10) - 1(x + 10) = 0$$
$$(x - 1)(x + 10) = 0$$

$x - 1 = 0$ or $x + 10 = 0$
$x = 1$ or $x = -10$

Quadratic formula

To solve quadratic equations of the form $ax^2 + bx + c = 0$ use the formula

$$x = \frac{-b \pm \sqrt{b^2 - 4ac}}{2a}$$

where a is the number in front of the x^2, b is the number in front of the x and c is the constant (number without an x).

Method

> **Step 1:** Write out clearly what a = , b = and c =.
> **Step 2:** Write down the formula.
> **Step 3:** Put figures into formula. Be careful with signs; remember a double minus is a plus.
> **Step 4:** Work out your answers. Remember to split the question into two, with one using plus sign and one using minus sign before the square root.

We use this formula in two types of question with quadratics:

(a) where double brackets or guide number does not work
(b) when the question asks to find x to two decimal places or in surd form.

Note: Some students are unable to factorise out a quadratic, so that means that they use the quadratic formula for every quadratic and that is a very good idea. It takes longer but at least you will pick up marks.

Example: Solve for $x^2 - 2x - 5 = 0$ and leave the answer in surd form.
Note: If we try to factorise using double brackets or guide number we cannot, so use the formula.

Solution

$a = 1$, $b = -2$ and $c = -5$

$$x = \frac{-b \pm \sqrt{b^2 - 4ac}}{2a}$$

sub the numbers in for letters

$$x = \frac{-(-2) \pm \sqrt{(-2)^2 - 4(1)(-5)}}{2(1)}$$

be very careful that $-4(1)(-5) = 20$

$$= \frac{2 \pm \sqrt{4 + 20}}{2}$$

$$= \frac{2 \pm \sqrt{24}}{2}$$

$$= \frac{2 \pm 2\sqrt{6}}{2} \quad \text{(note below)}$$

divide each term by 2

$$= 1 \pm \sqrt{6}$$

Note: We can use the rules of surds to simplify $\sqrt{24}$ into two separate surds.

$$\sqrt{24} = \sqrt{4}\sqrt{6}$$

$$= 2\sqrt{6}$$

Equations that become quadratics

The next 3 examples are difficult and have all being asked as (c) parts. Try not to be put off by how long they are, but work through them slowly and hope to get at least part of them right.

Example: Solve:

$$\frac{x-1}{x} - \frac{3x}{x-1} = 2, \quad x \neq 0 \text{ and } x \neq 1$$

Solution

$$\frac{x-1}{x} - \frac{3x}{x-1} = \frac{2}{1}$$

find a common denominator and change the top

$$\frac{(x-1)(x-1) - 3x(x)}{x(x-1)} = \frac{2x(x-1)}{x(x-1)}$$

$$(x-1)(x-1) - 3x(x) = 2x(x-1)$$

27

multiply out

$$x(x-1) - 1(x-1) - 3x^2 = 2x^2 - 2x$$

split the brackets and take your time

$$x^2 - x - x + 1 - 3x^2 = 2x^2 - 2x$$

tidy up each side

$$-2x^2 - 2x + 1 = 2x^2 - 2x$$

bring all terms to the left

$$-4x^2 + 1 = 0$$

change sign of whole line

$$4x^2 - 1 = 0$$

factorise using difference of two squares

$$(2x - 1)(2x + 1) = 0$$

$$2x - 1 = 0 \quad \text{or} \quad 2x + 1 = 0$$

$$2x = 1 \quad \text{or} \quad 2x = -1$$

$$x = \frac{1}{2} \quad \text{or} \quad x = -\frac{1}{2}$$

Example: Write $\frac{1}{x+1} + \frac{2}{x-3}$ as a single fraction where $x \neq -1$ and $x \neq 3$.

Hence, or otherwise, find, correct to one place of decimals, the two solutions of

$$\frac{1}{x+1} + \frac{2}{x-3} = 2, \quad x \neq -1 \text{ and } x \neq 3.$$

Solution

$$\frac{1}{x+1} + \frac{2}{x-3}$$

find a common denominator and change the top

$$\frac{1(x-3) + 2(x+1)}{(x+1)(x-3)}$$

change the top and tidy up

$$\frac{x - 3 + 2x + 2}{(x+1)(x-3)}$$

$$\frac{3x - 1}{(x+1)(x-3)}$$

But $\frac{1}{x+1} + \frac{2}{x-3} = 2$ (given)

so replace $\frac{1}{x+1} + \frac{2}{x-3}$ with

$\frac{3x-1}{(x+1)(x-3)}$ which we have done in part (i)

$$\frac{3x - 1}{(x+1)(x-3)} = \frac{2}{1}$$

find a common denominator

$$\frac{3x - 1 = 2(x+1)(x-3)}{(x+1)(x-3)}$$

multiply out top and drop the bottom (note below)

$$3x - 1 = 2x^2 - 4x - 6$$

all the terms to the left

$$3x - 1 - 2x^2 + 4x + 6 = 0$$

$$-2x^2 + 7x + 5 = 0$$

change sign of line (no minus in front of x^2)

$$2x^2 - 7x - 5 = 0$$

cannot factorise the quadratic so will need the quadratic formula

$a = 2, b = -7$ and $c = -5$

$$x = \frac{-b \pm \sqrt{b^2 - 4ac}}{2a}$$

$$x = \frac{-(-7) \pm \sqrt{(-7)^2 - 4(2)(-5)}}{2(2)}$$

sub in the numbers for letters

$$= \frac{7 \pm \sqrt{49 + 40}}{4}$$

28

the signs in front of the *y* are the same, so change signs of bottom line and add

$$2x + 2y = -8$$
$$-3x - 2y = 6$$
$$\overline{-x = -2}$$

change sign of the line

$$x = 2$$

Put $x = 2$ back into the top equation

$$2 + y = -4$$
$$y = -6$$

The answer is (2, –6).

Type 2

The intersection of a line and a curve

This is a really important section, as it comes up nearly every year both in the algebra questions and also in the circle question on paper 2. It is also difficult, so do not worry if you cannot get to an answer but try to at least get the first line right.

Example: Solve for *x* and *y*:

$$x + y = 3$$
$$x^2 + y^2 = 5$$

Solution

Step 1: Start with the equation that has no squares and write as either

$$x = \text{ or } y =$$
$$x + y = 3$$

leave the *x* on its own on the left-hand side

$$x = 3 - y$$

when a term crosses the equals it changes sign

Step 2: Sub $x = 3 - y$ into the circle $x^2 + y^2 = 5$

$$x^2 + y^2 = 5$$

replace the *x* and put in $3 - y$

$$(3 - y)^2 + y^2 = 5$$

square means multiplied by itself

$$(3 - y)(3 - y) + y^2 = 5$$

split the brackets and do not lose the y^2

$$3(3 - y) - y(3 - y) + y^2 = 5$$

multiply out

$$9 - 3y - 3y + y^2 + y^2 = 5$$

bring everything to left-hand side

$$9 - 6y + 2y^2 - 5 = 0$$

this has turned into a quadratic

$$2y^2 - 6y + 4 = 0$$

divide across by 2 to make life easier

$$y^2 - 3y + 2 = 0$$

nice easy quadratic

$$y^2 - 1y - 2y + 2 = 0$$

guide number of 3 and add to 2

$$y(y - 1) - 2(y - 1) = 0$$

take out what's common

$$(y - 1)(y - 2) = 0$$

let each bracket = 0

$$y - 1 = 0 \text{ or } y - 2 = 0$$
$$y = 1 \text{ or } \quad y = 2$$

Step 3: Sub $y = 1$ into the line $x = 3 - y$

$$x = 3 - 1$$
$$x = 2 \quad \text{one point is (2, 1)}$$

Sub $y = 2$ into the line $x = 3 - y$

$$x = 3 - 2$$
$$x = 1 \quad \text{other point is (1, 2)}$$

Points of intersection are (2, 1) and (1, 2).

Cubic equations

This comes down to either of two methods:

(a) sub in or   (b) divide in.

Type 1

Example: Show that $x = -3$ is a root of
$$x^3 - 2x^2 - 11x + 12 = 0.$$

Solution

Sub in $x = -3$ into the equation and the answer should equal 0.

$$(-3)^3 - 2(-3)^2 - 11(-3) + 12 = 0$$

powers first then multiply

$$-27 - 2(9) + 33 + 12 = 0$$
$$-27 - 18 + 33 + 12 = 0$$

Type 2

Example: Factorise $2x^3 - 5x^2 + x + 2 = 0$.

Solution

Sub in different values of x until we come up with an answer of 0.

Note: The first factor will always be a factor of the constant in the cubic.

Let $\quad f(x) = 2x^3 - 5x^2 + x + 2$

$$f(1) = 2(1)^3 - 5(1)^2 + 1 + 2$$

powers first then multiply

$$= 2 - 5 + 1 + 2 = 0$$

$x = 1$ is a root, so $x - 1$ is a factor. To find the other factors then divide in by $x - 1$.

$$
\begin{array}{r}
2x^2 - 3x - 2 \\
x - 1 \overline{\smash{\big)}\, 2x^3 - 5x^2 + x + 2} \\
\underline{2x^3 - 2x^2} \quad \text{change the sign}\\
-3x^2 + x \\
\underline{-3x^2 + 3x} \quad \text{change the sign}\\
-2x + 2 \\
\underline{-2x + 2} \\
0
\end{array}
$$

Factors are $(x - 1)(2x^2 - 3x - 2)$
$ = (x - 1)(2x + 1)(x - 2)$

Note: To do long division: Divide first into first, put answer on top. Multiply top by side and put answer underneath. Change the sign of the line and add. Keep going.

Type 3

Example: One unknown variable in cubic
If $x + 2$ is a factor of $x^3 - 3x + k = 0$, find the value of k and the other two roots.

Solution

Since $x + 2$ is a factor then can sub in $x = -2$ and answer must equal 0.

$$f(-2) = (-2)^3 - 3(-2) + k = 0$$
$$-8 + 6 + k = 0$$
$$k = 2$$

Note: When we are given a cubic equation that has only three terms, make it into four by putting in $0x^2$ (as in the above example)

$$
\begin{array}{r}
x^2 - 2x + 1 \\
x + 2 \overline{\smash{\big)}\, x^3 + 0x^2 - 3x + 2} \\
\underline{x^3 + 2x^2} \\
-2x^2 - 3x \\
\underline{-2x^2 - 4x} \\
x + 2 \\
\underline{x + 2} \\
0
\end{array}
$$

Solve quadratic $x^2 - 2x + 1 = 0$ to find $x = 1$ or $x = 1$.

Type 4

Example: Two unknown variables in cubic

If $f(x) = 2x^3 + ax^2 + bx + 2$, where a and b are real numbers, given that $x - 1$ and $x - 2$ are factors of $f(x)$, find the values of a and b.

Solution

Sub $x = 2$ and $x = 1$ into the equation $f(x) = 2x^3 + ax^2 + bx + 2$ to be left with two equations in terms of a and b.
When $x = 2$:

$$f(2) = 2(2)^3 + a(2)^2 + b(2) + 2 = 0$$

replace x with 2

$$2(8) + 4a + 2b + 2 = 0$$

powers first then multiply

$$16 + 4a + 2b + 2 = 0 \quad \text{tidy up}$$

$$4a + 2b + 18 = 0$$

divide every term by 2

$$2a + b = -9$$

leave letters on left, numbers on right.

Note: Because there are two unknowns you should realise that we need a second equation, so that we sub in $x = 1$ and solve the simultaneous equations

$$f(1) = 2(1)^3 + a(1)^2 + b(1) + 2 = 0$$

$$2 + a + b + 2 = 0$$

$$a + b + 4 = 0$$

$$a + b = -4$$

$$\begin{aligned} 2a + b &= -9 \\ a + b &= -4 \quad \text{change sign of line} \\ \hline a &= -5 \end{aligned}$$

Put $a = -5$ back into the second equation

$$-5 + b = -4$$

$$b = 1$$

Indices

The first thing to do here is to learn off the rules of indices.

Rule 1: $a^m \times a^n = a^{m+n}$	$a^{m+n} = a^m \times a^n$
Rule 2: $\dfrac{a^m}{a^n} = a^{m-n}$	$a^{m-n} = \dfrac{a^m}{a^n}$
Rule 3: $a^0 = 1$	$1 = a^0$
Rule 4: $\dfrac{1}{a^m} = a^{-m}$	$a^{-m} = \dfrac{1}{a^m}$
Rule 5: $(a^m)^n = a^{mn}$	$a^{mn} = (a^m)^n$
Rule 6: $a^{\frac{1}{n}} = \sqrt[n]{a}$	$\sqrt[n]{a} = a^{\frac{1}{n}}$

backwards the rules are

You must know the rules in both directions.

Type 1

Evaluations

Example: Find the value of 2^3 and $27^{-2/3}$ leaving the answer in the form $\dfrac{a}{b}$.

Solution

$2^3 = 8$ do not make mistake that $2^3 = 6$

On the calculator put in $\boxed{2}$, then use the $\boxed{x^y}$ button, then $\boxed{3}$ $\boxed{=}$ $\boxed{8}$

$$27^{-2/3} = \frac{1}{27^{2/3}} = \frac{1}{(27^{1/3})^2} = \frac{1}{3^2} = \frac{1}{9}$$

on the calculator put in $\boxed{27}$, then use the $\boxed{x^y}$ button, then $\boxed{2}$, then $\boxed{a^b/c}$, then $\boxed{3}$, then $\boxed{\pm}$.

33

Type 2

x in the powers

Example: Find the value of *x* in each of the following:

(i) $8^x = \dfrac{16}{\sqrt{2}}$

(ii) $25^x = \dfrac{1}{125}$

Solution

The main idea is to change all the numbers to the same base and then use the rules of indices to have one power = one power, so that the powers must be equal.

(i) $8^x = \dfrac{16}{\sqrt{2}}$ change to the base 2

$(2^3)^x = \dfrac{2^4}{2^{1/2}}$

use rules of indices:

$(a^m)^n = a^{mn}$ and $\dfrac{a^m}{a^n} = a^{m-n}$

$2^{3x} = 2^{4-1/2}$

$2^{3x} = 2^{3^{1/2}}$ tidy up

$3x = 3\dfrac{1}{2}$ drop the base

$3x = 3.5$ change into a decimal

$x = 1.166$ divide by 3

(ii) $25^x = \dfrac{1}{125}$

$(5^2)^x = \dfrac{1}{5^3}$ change to base 5

use rules of indices:

$(a^m)^n = a^{mn}$ and $\dfrac{1}{a^m} = a^{-m}$

$5^{2x} = 5^{-3}$

$2x = -3$ drop the base

$x = -\dfrac{3}{2}$ divide across by 2

Chapter 3
Complex Numbers

Contents

(a) Notation (page 35)
(b) To add or subtract (page 36)
(c) Multiplication of complex numbers (page 36)
(d) Complex conjugates (page 37)
(e) Division (page 37)
(f) Argand diagram (page 38)
(g) Modulus (page 38)
(h) Equality (page 39)
(i) Quadratics (page 41).

Notation

Example: Solve the equation
$z^2 - 4z + 5 = 0$.

Solution
This is a quadratic equation where we need the quadratic formula to solve it, as from algebra.

Write down the values of a, b and c
$$a = 1, b = -4, c = 5$$
write down the formula
$$z = \frac{-b \pm \sqrt{b^2 - 4ac}}{2a}$$
put the figures in
$$= \frac{-(-4) \pm \sqrt{(-4)^2 - 4(1)(5)}}{2(1)}$$

multiply first, then add and subtract
$$= \frac{4 \pm \sqrt{16 - 20}}{2}$$
$$= \frac{4 \pm \sqrt{-4}}{2}$$

can split the square root up $\sqrt{ab} = \sqrt{a}\sqrt{b}$
$$= \frac{4 \pm \sqrt{4}\sqrt{-1}}{2} \qquad \sqrt{-1} = i$$
$$= \frac{4 \pm 2i}{2}$$
$$= 2 \pm i$$

The real part of $2 + i$ is 2 and the imaginary part is i.
The real part of $2 - i$ is 2 and the imaginary part is $-i$.

A complex number is usually denoted by z and is said to be of the form $z = a + bi$.

z has two parts:
the real part called Re(z), which is a
the imaginary part Im(z), which is given by bi.

$i = \sqrt{-1}$
$i^2 = -1$

Example: Given that $i^2 = -1$, find the value of:

(a) i^9

(b) i^{10}

Solution

Use the rules of indices to split the power up using i^2

(a) $i^9 = i^2 i^2 i^2 i^2 i$

　　　$= (-1)(-1)(-1)(-1)i$ since $i^2 = -1$

　　　$= i$

(b) $i^{10} = i^2 i^2 i^2 i^2 i^2$

　　　$= (-1)(-1)(-1)(-1)(-1)$

　　　$= -1$

To add or subtract complex numbers

Add real to real and imaginary to imaginary.

Example: If $z_1 = 2 + 4i$ and $z_2 = 3 - 5i$, find the values of:

(i) $z_1 + z_2$
(ii) $6z_1 - 7z_2$

Solution

(i) $z_1 + z_2 = 2 + 4i + 3 - 5i$

　　　add $2 + 3$ and $4i - 5i$

　　　$= 5 - i$

(ii) $6z_1 - 7z_2 = 6(2 + 4i) - 7(3 - 5i)$

　　　multiply out the brackets

　　　$= 12 + 24i - 21 + 35i$

　　　add real to real and imaginary to imaginary

　　　$= -9 + 59i$

Multiplication of complex numbers

Same method as in algebra. One very important point is that $i^2 = -1$.

Example: If $z = 3 - i$ and $w = 5 + 2i$, simplify each of the following:

(i) iz
(ii) zw

Solution

(i) $iz = i(3 - i)$

multiply everything inside by what's outside

　　　$= 3i - i^2$ but $i^2 = -1$

　　　$= 3i - (-1)$

be careful of double minus signs

　　　$= 3i + 1$

normally finish by putting real number first

　　　$= 1 + 3i$

(ii) $zw = (3 - i)(5 + 2i)$

split the first bracket and write second one twice

　　　$= 3(5 + 2i) - i(5 + 2i)$

multiply everything inside by what's outside

　　　$= 15 + 6i - 5i - 2i^2$ but $i^2 = -1$

　　　$= 15 + i - 2(-1)$

　　　$= 15 + i + 2$

　　　$= 17 + i$

Complex conjugates

If $z = a + bi$ then the conjugate is written $\bar{z} = a - bi$. That is, change the sign of the imaginary part.

Example: If $z = 3 + 5i$, find the value of $z\bar{z}$.

Solution

$$z = 3 + 5i$$
$$\bar{z} = 3 - 5i$$

Note: $z\bar{z}$ means multiply $z = 3 + 5i$ by its conjugate $\bar{z} = 3 - 5i$, as above.

$z\bar{z} = (3 + 5i)(3 - 5i)$ split the brackets

$$= 3(3 - 5i) + 5i(3 - 5i)$$
$$= 9 - 15i + 15i - 25i^2$$

remember $i^2 = -1$

$$= 9 - 25(-1)$$
$$= 9 + 25 = 34$$

Division by a complex number

Multiply above and below by the complex conjugate of the bottom.

Example: Write $\dfrac{z_1}{z_2}$ in the form $a + bi$, where $z_1 = 4 + 3i$ and $z_2 = 2 - 5i$.

Solution

$$\frac{z_1}{z_2} = \frac{4 + 3i}{2 - 5i}$$

multiply above and below by $2 + 5i$

$$\frac{z_1}{z_2} = \frac{4 + 3i}{2 - 5i} \cdot \frac{2 + 5i}{2 + 5i}$$

Separate the question:
Multiply the top by top and then the bottom by bottom and put the two answers back over each other.

Top by top:

$$(4 + 3i)(2 + 5i) \quad \text{split the brackets}$$
$$= 4(2 + 5i) + 3i(2 + 5i)$$
$$= 8 + 20i + 6i + 15i^2 \quad \text{but } i^2 = -1$$
$$= 8 + 26i - 15$$

add real to real and imaginary to imaginary

$$= -7 + 26i$$

bottom by bottom:

$$(2 - 5i)(2 + 5i)$$
$$= 2(2 + 5i) - 5i(2 + 5i)$$
$$= 4 + 10i - 10i - 25i^2$$
$$= 4 + 25 = 29$$

$$\text{Answer} = \frac{-7 + 26i}{29}$$

Example: If $w = 2 + 2i$, simplify $\dfrac{1}{w + 4}$.

Solution

$$\frac{1}{w + 4} = \frac{1}{2 + 2i + 4}$$

sub in the value of w and simplify the bottom

$$= \frac{1}{6 + 2i}$$

multiply above and below by $6 - 2i$

$$= \frac{1}{6 + 2i} \cdot \frac{6 - 2i}{6 - 2i}$$

top by top:

$$(1)(6 - 2i) = 6 - 2i$$

bottom by bottom:

$(6 + 2i)(6 - 2i)$ split the brackets

$$= 6(6 - 2i) + 2i(6 - 2i)$$
$$= 36 - 12i + 12i - 4i^2$$

remember $i^2 = -1$ and watch the signs

$$= 36 - 4(-1)$$
$$= 36 + 4 = 40$$

Answer $= \dfrac{6 - 2i}{40}$

divide above and below by 2

$$= \dfrac{3 - i}{20}$$

Argand diagram

Same as x- and y-axes in coordinate geometry.
The x-axis is now the real axis.
The y-axis is now the imaginary axis.

Example: Let $w = 1 + 2i$.
Plot on an Argand diagram
(a) w
(b) $\overline{w}$, where $\overline{w}$ is the conjugate of w
(c) iw
(d) $w + 3$

Solution
(a) $w = 1 + 2i$
(b) $\overline{w} = 1 - 2i$
(c) $iw = i(1 + 2i) = i + 2i^2$ but $i^2 = -1$
$$= i + 2(-1)$$
$$= -2 + i$$

(d) $w + 3 = 1 + 2i + 3 = 4 + 2i$

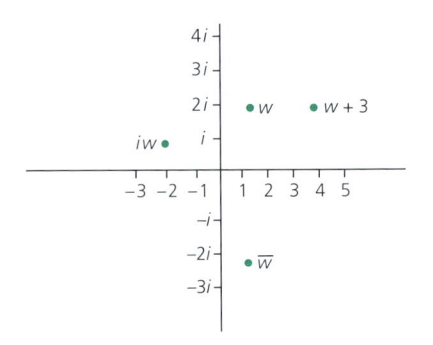

Modulus

This is the distance of the complex number from the origin.
If $z = a + bi$, then the modulus of z (written as $|z|$) is given by the formula

$$|z| = \sqrt{a^2 + b^2}$$

Example: Find $|z_1|$ and $|z_2|$. Hence, show that $|z_1 z_2| = |z_1||z_2|$ where $z_1 = 3 - 5i$ and $z_2 = 1 - 2i$.

Solution

When $z = a + bi$ then $|z| = \sqrt{a^2 + b^2}$

$z_1 = 3 - 5i$ so $|z| = \sqrt{a^2 + b^2}$

$$|z_1| = \sqrt{3^2 + (-5)^2}$$
$$= \sqrt{9 + 25} = \sqrt{34}$$

$$|z_2| = \sqrt{1^2 + (-2)^2}$$
$$= \sqrt{1 + 4} = \sqrt{5}$$

$|z_1 z_2| = |z_1||z_2|$. What is the difference between the left and the right sides?
On the left we need to multiply the two

complex numbers by each other and then get the modulus. On the right we need to get the modulus of each of the numbers and then multiply the two answers.

$z_1 z_2 = (3 - 5i)(1 - 2i)$ split the brackets

$= 3(1 - 2i) - 5i(1 - 2i)$

$= 3 - 6i - 5i + 10i^2$

$= 3 - 11i + 10(-1)$

$= 3 - 11i - 10$

$= -7 - 11i$

$|z_1 z_2| = \sqrt{(-7)^2 + (-11)^2}$

$= \sqrt{49 + 121}$

$= \sqrt{170}$

Use the calculator to prove that

$|z_1 z_2| = |z_1||z_2|$

$\sqrt{170} = \sqrt{34}\sqrt{5}$

$13.038 = (5.83)(2.236)$

$13.038 = 13.038$ true

Example: If $z = 4 + ki$ and $|z| = 5$ find two values of k, where $k \in R$.

Solution

When $z = a + bi$ then $|z| = \sqrt{a^2 + b^2}$

$|z| = \sqrt{4^2 + k^2} = 5$

square both sides

$16 + k^2 = 25$

$k^2 = 9$

$k = \pm 3$

(when we take the root of a number, the answer = ±)

Example: If $z = 2 + i$ and $w = 3 - 6i$ find the value of k, where $k \in R$, if $|w| = k|z|$.

Solution

$|z| = \sqrt{2^2 + 1^2}$

$= \sqrt{4 + 1} = \sqrt{5}$

$|w| = \sqrt{3^2 + (-6)^2}$

$= \sqrt{9 + 36} = \sqrt{45}$

$|w| = k|z|$

sub in $|z| = \sqrt{5}$ and $|w| = \sqrt{45}$

$\sqrt{45} = k\sqrt{5}$

swap sides so that the letters are on the left

$k\sqrt{5} = \sqrt{45}$

divide across by $\sqrt{5}$

$k = \dfrac{\sqrt{45}}{\sqrt{5}}$

use the calculator to come up with the answer

$= 3$

Equality of complex numbers

If two complex numbers are equal, then real equals real and imaginary equals imaginary.

Note: This is important for (c)-type questions and is really worth putting a lot of effort into, as it is not the worst (c) part. We use this idea when we have equals in the question and unknown letters.

Example:
If $k(2 + 3i) + l(-3 + i) = -4 + 5i$, find the value of k and the value of l.

Solution
Multiply out and then let the real equal the real and the imaginary equal the imaginary.

$$k(2 + 3i) + l(-3 + i) = -4 + 5i$$

multiply out

$$2k + 3ki - 3l + li = -4 + 5i$$

real equals the real

$$2k - 3l = -4$$

imaginary equals the imaginary

$$3k + l = 5$$

Solve the simultaneous equations:

$$2k - 3l = -4$$
$$9k + 3l = 15 \quad \text{multiply bottom line by 3}$$
$$\overline{}$$
$$11k = 11$$
$$k = 1$$

Sub $k = 1$ into $3k + l = 5$ to get $l = 2$.

Example: Let $z = 1 + i$ and let $\bar{z}$ be the conjugate of z.

Express $\dfrac{z}{\bar{z}}$ in the form $x + yi$, $x, y \in R$.

Hence solve

$k\left(\dfrac{z}{\bar{z}}\right) + tz = -3 - 4i$ for real k and real t.

Solution

$$z = 1 + i$$
$$\bar{z} = 1 - i$$

that is, change the sign of the imaginary part.

$$\frac{z}{\bar{z}} = \frac{1 + i}{1 - i}$$

multiply above and below by $1 + i$, the conjugate of the bottom

$$\frac{1 + i}{1 - i} \cdot \frac{1 + i}{1 + i}$$

top by top:

$$(1 + i)(1 + i)$$
$$1(1 + i) + i(1 + i)$$
$$1 + i + i + i^2$$
$$1 + 2i - 1$$
$$2i$$

bottom by bottom:

$$(1 - i)(1 + i)$$
$$1(1 + i) - i(1 + i)$$
$$1 + i - i - i^2$$
$$1 - (-1)$$
$$1 + 1 = 2$$

$$\frac{z}{\bar{z}} = \frac{1 + i}{1 - i} \cdot \frac{1 + i}{1 + i} = \frac{2i}{2} = i$$

$$k\left(\frac{z}{\bar{z}}\right) + tz = -3 - 4i$$

$$ki + t(1 + i) = -3 - 4i$$

$$ki + t + ti = -3 - 4i$$

real equals the real

$$t = -3$$

imaginary equals the imaginary

$$k + t = -4$$
$$k - 3 = -4$$
$$k = -4 + 3$$
$$k = -1$$

Quadratics

Example: Show that $2 - i$ is a root of $z^2 - 4z + 5 = 0$ and state the other root.

Solution

To show it is a root replace z with $2 - i$ and work out; the answer should be 0.

$$z^2 - 4z + 5 = 0$$

replace z with $2 - i$

$$(2 - i)^2 - 4(2 - i) + 5 = 0$$
$$2(2 - i) - i(2 - i) - 8 + 4i + 5 = 0$$
$$4 - 2i - 2i + i^2 - 8 + 4i + 5 = 0$$
$$4 - 4i - 1 - 8 + 4i + 5 = 0$$
$$0 = 0$$

(since $4 - 1 - 8 + 5 = 0$ and $-4i + 4i = 0$)

The other root is the complex conjugate, namely $2 + i$.

Example: If $1 + 3i$ is a root of $x^2 + hx + k = 0$, find the value of h and the value of k.

Solution

Replace x with $1 + 3i$ and then let real equal real and imaginary equal imaginary.

$$x^2 + hx + k = 0$$

sub in $x = 2 + i$

$$(1 + 3i)^2 + h(1 + 3i) + k = 0$$

must square out

$$(1 + 3i)^2 = (1 + 3i)(1 + 3i)$$
$$(1 + 3i)(1 + 3i) + h(1 + 3i) + k = 0$$
$$1(1 + 3i) + 3i(1 + 3i) + h(1 + 3i) + k = 0$$
$$1 + 3i + 3i + 9i^2 + h + 3hi + k = 0$$
$$1 + 6i - 9 + h + 3hi + k = 0$$
$$-8 + 6i + h + 3hi + k = 0$$

let real equal and imaginary equal imaginary

Imaginary has only one unknown, so work it out first.

Imaginary equals imaginary

$$6 + 3h = 0$$

letters to left, numbers to right

$$3h = -6$$
$$h = -2$$

Real equals real

$$-8 + h + k = 0 \quad \text{sub in } h = -2$$
$$-8 - 2 + k = 0$$
$$-10 + k = 0$$
$$k = 10$$

Chapter 4
Sequences and Series

Contents

(a) Definitions of sequences and series (page 42)
(b) Arithmetic sequences and series (page 43)
(c) Geometric sequences and series (page 46)
(d) Given S_n: to find T_n (page 49).

Definitions of sequences and series

Sequence: a set of numbers or an algebraic expression defined by some mathematical *rule*.

Example: Find the next 3 terms of the following sequences:

(i)   2, 5, 8, - - -
(ii) 3, 12, 48, - - -

Solution

(i) From the first 3 terms, can you see any pattern that you must continue? You have to see if there is any common addition or common multiplication from one term to the next. It has to be one or the other.

2, 5, 8: can you see that to get from one term to the next we have added 3? So continue the pattern:

2, 5, 8, 11, 14, 17

(ii) 3, 12, 48: try to see if there is any common addition. 3 to 12 add 9, 12 to 48 add 36; so this is not the same. This one must be about common multiplication.

3 by 4 is 12, 12 by 4 is 48, 48 by 4 is 192; to get from one term to the next multiply by 4.

3, 12, 48, 192, 768, 3072.

Individual terms of the sequence are denoted by the letter T or U with a subscript.

$$T_4 - 4^{\text{th}} \text{ term}$$

$$U_{17} - 17^{\text{th}} \text{ term.}$$

Term = an element of a sequence, i.e. it is one part of the sequence.

Series: from each sequence we can construct a series S_n as follows:

$$S_n = T_1 + T_2 + T_3 + \text{- - -} + T_n$$

Note: A series is the addition of all the terms of a sequence. It is denoted by the letter S with a subscript.

$$S_4 = T_1 + T_2 + T_3 + T_4$$

Example: If $U_n = 3n - 5$, find the values of:
- (i) U_1
- (ii) U_4

Solution

(i) To find U_1 replace every n with 1.
$$U_1 = 3(1) - 5$$
$$= 3 - 5 = -2$$

(ii) To find U_4 replace every n with 4.
$$U_4 = 3(4) - 5$$
$$= 12 - 5 = 7$$

Example: If $T_n = 5n - 7$, find the value of n for which $T_n = 48$.

Solution

Let $T_n = T_n$ and solve the equation
$$5n - 7 = 48$$
$$5n = 55$$
$$n = 11$$

Arithmetic sequences and series

There are 6 types of question here.

Type 1

A sequence which obeys the rule $T_{n+1} - T_n$ constant is called an **arithmetic sequence.**

To get from one term to the next we add (or subtract) the same number each time.

Example: Prove that the sequence $T_n = 4n + 3$ is arithmetic.

Solution
$$T_n = 4n + 3$$
replace the n with $n + 1$
$$T_{n+1} = 4(n + 1) + 3$$
multiply out the bracket and add
$$= 4n + 4 + 3$$
$$= 4n + 7$$
$$T_{n+1} - T_n = 4n + 7 - (4n + 3)$$
be very careful with the minus sign
$$= 4n + 7 - 4n - 3$$
$$= 4$$

4 is a constant, so the sequence is arithmetic.

Type 2

The first term is denoted by a, so $a = T_1$

The constant is called the **common difference** and is denoted by d, so $d = T_2 - T_1$

Example: The first term of an arithmetic sequence is 30 and the common difference is –3. Write down the first five terms of the sequence.

Solution

Start with 30 and keep on adding –3 to each term:
$$30, 27, 24, 21, 18$$

43

Example: The first three terms of an arithmetic sequence are 4.5, 6, 7.5. Find a, the first term, and d, the common difference.

Solution

$$a = T_1 = 4.5$$
$$d = T_2 - T_1 = 6 - 4.5 = 1.5$$

Example: The nth term of an arithmetic series is given by $T_n = 4n - 2$.
The first term is a and the common difference is d. Find the value of a and the value of d.

Solution

$$a = T_1$$

sub in $n = 1$. Multiply first then subtract

$$T_1 = 4(1) - 2$$
$$= 4 - 2 = 2$$

sub in $n = 2$. Multiply first then subtract

$$T_2 = 4(2) - 2$$
$$= 8 - 2 = 6$$
$$d = T_2 - T_1$$
$$= 6 - 2 = 4$$

Type 3

The general term of an arithmetic sequence T_n is given by
$T_n = a + (n - 1)d$.

Example: The first three terms of an arithmetic sequence are 5, 8, 11. Find T_n the nth term, and hence find T_{12}.

Solution

$$a = 5$$
$$d = T_2 - T_1 = 8 - 5 = 3$$

General term is given by $T_n = a + (n - 1)d$
sub in $a = 5$ and $d = 3$

$$T_n = 5 + (n - 1)3$$

switch the 3 in front of brackets and then multiply

$$= 5 + 3(n - 1)$$
$$= 5 + 3n - 3$$
$$= 3n + 2$$
$$T_{12} = 3(12) + 2$$
$$= 36 + 2 = 38$$

Example: The first term of an arithmetic sequence is 7 and the common difference is –2. Which term of the sequence is –351?

Solution

Write down what we know from the question: $a = 7$ and $d = -2$.
We are asked to find which term has a value of –351; since we do not know which term this is we let $T_n = -351$.

$T_n = a + (n - 1)d$ sub in $a = 7$, $d = -2$
and $T_n = -351$ to find the value of n.

$$-351 = 7 + (n - 1)(-2)$$

switch –2 in front of bracket

$$-351 = 7 - 2(n - 1)$$

multiply out and watch for signs

$$-351 = 7 - 2n + 2$$
$$-351 = 9 - 2n$$

switch both sides so that the letters are on left

$$9 - 2n = -351$$

solve the equation

$$-2n = -360$$
$$2n = 360$$
$$n = 180$$

Type 4

Example: The sixth term of an arithmetic sequence is 13 and the tenth term is 5. Find the first term and the common difference.

Look at the information we have and see which formula we can use.

Solution

We know that $T_6 = 13$ and $T_{10} = 5$.

Since we know the value of two terms we can use the T_n formula twice.
$T_n = a + (n - 1)d$

$$T_6 = a + 5d = 13$$
$$T_{10} = a + 9d = 5$$

Solve the simultaneous equations.

$$a + 5d = 13$$
$$\underline{a + 9d = 5}$$

change sign of the bottom line

$$-4d = 8$$
$$d = -2$$

Sub $d = -2$ into $a + 5d = 13$

$$a + 5d = 13$$
$$a + 5(-2) = 13$$
$$a - 10 = 13$$
$$a = 23$$

Type 5

The sum of the first n terms of an arithmetic series S_n is given by

$S_n = \frac{n}{2}\{2a + (n - 1)d\}$.

Example: Find S_n and S_{12} of
$6 + 2 - 2 - 6 - - -$

Solution

$$a = 6$$
$$d = T_2 - T_1 = 2 - 6 = -4$$
$$S_n = \frac{n}{2}\{2a + (n - 1)d\}$$

sub in $a = 6$ and $d = -4$

$$= \frac{n}{2}\{2(6) + (n - 1)(-4)\}$$

swap the –4 in front of the brackets

$$= \frac{n}{2}\{2(6) - 4(n - 1)\}$$

multiply out

$$= \frac{n}{2}\{12 - 4n + 4\}$$

$$= \frac{n}{2}\{16 - 4n\}$$

$$S_{12} = \frac{12}{2}\{16 - 4(12)\} \text{ sub in } n = 12$$

$$= 6(16 - 48)$$
$$= 6(-32) = -192$$

Example: The first term of an arithmetic sequence is –4 and the common difference is 2.

How many terms of the series must be added to give a sum of 126?

Solution

Write down what we know from the question: $a = -4$ and $d = 2$.

We are asked to find how many terms must be added to give an answer of 126, so we let $S_n = 126$.

$$S_n = \frac{n}{2}\{2a + (n - 1)d\}$$

sub in $a = -4$, $d = 2$ and $S_n = 126$

$$126 = \frac{n}{2}\{2(-4) + (n-1)(2)\}$$

swap the 2 in front of brackets

$$126 = \frac{n}{2}\{-8 + 2(n-1)\}$$

multiply out

$$126 = \frac{n}{2}\{-8 + 2n - 2\}$$

tidy up

$$126 = \frac{n}{2}(2n - 10)$$

divide by the 2

$$126 = n(n-5)$$

multiply out to form a quadratic which we solve

$$126 = n^2 - 5n$$
$$n^2 - 5n - 126 = 0$$
$$(n-14)(n+9) = 0$$
$$n - 14 = 0 \text{ or } n + 9 = 0$$
$$n = 14 \quad n = -9$$

Since we are asked to find the number of terms, the only possible answer is $n = 14$.

Type 6

Example: The first three terms in an arithmetic sequence are $x - 3$, $2x + 7$ and $x + 5$. Find the value of x.

Solution

Here we use the idea that $\boxed{T_3 - T_2 = T_2 - T_1}$

$T_1 = x - 3$
$T_2 = 2x + 7$
$T_3 = x + 5$

$$2x + 7 - (x - 3) = x + 5 - (2x + 7)$$
$$2x + 7 - x + 3 = x + 5 - 2x - 7$$
$$x + 10 = -x - 2$$
$$2x = -12$$
$$x = -6$$

Geometric sequences and series

There are 6 types of question here.

Type 1

A sequence that obeys the rule

$$\frac{T_{n+1}}{T_n} = \text{constant}$$

is called a geometric sequence.

To get from one term to the next we multiply (or divide) by the same number each time.

Example: Prove that the sequence $T_n = 3^n$ is geometric.

Solution

$$T_n = 3^n$$
$$T_{n+1} = 3^{n+1}$$
$$\frac{T_{n+1}}{T_n} = \frac{3^{n+1}}{3^n}$$

use the rules of indices to subtract the powers

$$= 3^{n+1-n} = 3$$

3 is a constant, so the sequence is geometric.

Type 2

> The first term is denoted by a, so $a = T_1$

> The number we multiply by is called the **common ratio** and is denoted by r, where $r = \dfrac{T_2}{T_1}$

Example: The first term of a geometric sequence is 5 and the common ratio is 2. Write down the first five terms of the sequence.

Solution

Start with 5 and keep on multiplying each term by 2:

$$5, 10, 20, 40, 80$$

Example: The first three terms of a geometric sequence are 4, –12, 36. Find a, the first term, and r, the common ratio.

Solution

$$a = T_1 = 4$$

$$r = \dfrac{T_2}{T_1} = \dfrac{-12}{4} = -3$$

Example: The nth term of a geometric series is given by $T_n = 5(2)^n$.
  The first term is a and the common ratio is r. Find the value of a and the value of r.

Solution

$$a = T_1$$

$$T_1 = 5(2)^1 \quad \text{sub in } n = 1$$

$$= 5(2) = 10$$

$$T_2 = 5(2)^2 \quad \text{sub in } n = 2; \text{ square first then multiply}$$

$$= 5(4) = 20$$

$$r = \dfrac{T_2}{T_1}$$

$$= \dfrac{20}{10} = 2$$

Type 3

> The general term of a geometric sequence, T_n, is given by $T_n = ar^{n-1}$

Example: The first three terms of a geometric sequence are 5, –15, 45. Find T_n, the nth term, and hence find T_8.

Solution

The first term $T_1 = a = 5$

$$r = \dfrac{T_2}{T_1}$$

$$= \dfrac{-15}{5} = -3$$

$$T_n = ar^{n-1}$$

sub in $a = 5$ and $r = -3$

$$= 5(-3)^{n-1}$$

Note: We cannot multiply $5(-3)^{n-1}$ since there is a power on the –3, so just leave it alone.

$$T_8 = 5(-3)^{8-1} \quad \text{sub in } n = 8$$

$$= 5(-3)^7 \quad \text{on calculator evaluate } (-3)^7$$

$$= 5(-2187) = -10935$$

Note: To calculate $(-3)^7$ use the calculator by entering $\boxed{3}\ \boxed{\pm}\ \boxed{y^x}\ \boxed{7}\ \boxed{=}$.

Type 4

Example: The fourth term of a geometric sequence is 36 and the sixth term is 144. Find the first term and the common ratio r, where $r > 0$.

Solution

$$T_4 = ar^3 = 36$$

$$T_6 = ar^5 = 144$$

from the first equation divide across by r^3

$$a = \frac{36}{r^3}$$

sub $a = r^3$ into the second equation and use rules of indices to simplify

$$\left(\frac{36}{r^3}\right)r^5 = 144$$

$$36r^2 = 144$$

divide across by 36

$$r^2 = 4$$

to get rid of the square take square root of both sides

$$r = 2$$

To find a sub $r = 2$ into $ar^3 = 36$

$$a(2)^3 = 36$$

cube first and solve the equation

$$8a = 36$$

$$a = 4.5$$

Type 5

The sum of the first n terms of a geometric series S_n is given by

$$S_n = \frac{a(1 - r^n)}{1 - r}$$

Example: The first three terms of a geometric sequence are 2, 6, 18.

(i) Write down the value of a and the value of r.
(ii) Find S_8, the sum of the first 8 terms.

Solution

(i) $a = T_1 = 2$

$$r = \frac{T_2}{T_1} = \frac{6}{2} = 3$$

(ii) $$S_n = \frac{a(1 - r^n)}{1 - r}$$

sub in $a = 2$, $r = 3$ and $n = 8$

$$S_8 = \frac{2(1 - 3^8)}{1 - 3}$$

$$= \frac{2(1 - 3^8)}{-2}$$

divide 2 by -2 and evaluate 3^8

$$= -(1 - 6561)$$

$$= -(-6560) = 6560$$

Type 6

Example: Find the values of x for which 2, $x + 1$, 32 are the first three terms in a geometric sequence.

Solution

Here we use the idea that $\boxed{\dfrac{T_2}{T_1} = \dfrac{T_3}{T_2}}$

$$T_1 = 2$$

$$T_2 = x + 1$$

$$T_3 = 32$$

$$\frac{x + 1}{2} = \frac{32}{x + 1}$$

48

get a common denominator
$$\frac{(x+1)(x+1) = 2(32)}{2(x+1)}$$

drop the bottom
$$x(x+1) + 1(x+1) = 64$$

multiply out top and solve the quadratic
$$x^2 + x + x + 1 = 64$$
$$x^2 + 2x - 63 = 0$$
$$(x+9)(x-7) = 0$$
$$x+9 = 0 \quad \text{or} \quad x-7 = 0$$
$$x = -9 \quad\quad\quad x = 7$$

Given S_n: to find T_n

Can use the idea that $\boxed{T_{10} = S_{10} - S_9}$

Example: S_n of an arithmetic series is given by $S_n = n^2 + 4n$. Find a, S_{10}, S_9 and hence find T_{10}.

Solution

$$\boxed{a = T_1 = S_1}$$

Sub in $n = 1$ and evaluate
$$S_1 = (1)^2 + 4(1)$$
$$= 1 + 4 = 5$$

sub in $n = 10$ and evaluate
$$S_{10} = (10)^2 + 4(10)$$
$$= 100 + 40 = 140$$

sub in $n = 9$ and evaluate
$$S_9 = (9)^2 + 4(9)$$
$$= 81 + 36 = 117$$
$$T_{10} = S_{10} - S_9$$
$$= 140 - 117 = 23$$

Example: If S_n of an arithmetic series is given by $S_n = n^2 - 3n$, find a and d.

Solution
$$a = T_1 = S_1$$

Sub in $n = 1$ and evaluate
$$S_1 = (1)^2 - 3(1)$$
$$= 1 - 3 = -2$$

To find d requires a little bit more knowledge.
$$d = T_2 - T_1$$

but we have been given S_n, so we need to find T_2.
$$T_2 = S_2 - S_1$$

sub in $n = 2$ and evaluate
$$S_2 = (2)^2 - 3(2)$$
$$= 4 - 6 = -2$$
$$T_2 = S_2 - S_1$$
$$= -2 - (-2)$$
$$= -2 + 2 = 0$$
$$d = T_2 - T_1$$
$$= 0 - (-2)$$
$$= 0 + 2 = 2$$

49

Chapter 5
Calculus and Differentiation

Contents

(a) Differentiation from first principles (page 50)
(b) Rules of differentiation (page 51)
(c) Evaluating derivatives (page 52)
(d) Product and quotient rules (pages 52–53)
(e) Chain rule (page 54)
(f) Equation of a tangent (page 54)
(g) Max and min and graphs (page 57)
(h) Speed and acceleration (page 60).

This is Question 7 on Paper One, but it is also a part of Question 6 and Question 8 so some knowledge of it is important.

Differentiation from first principles

There are two ways of doing this. Pick one and practise at it over and over, as this is a very common question.

Notation 1

Step 1: Let y = what is to be differentiated.
Step 2: Replace y with $y + \Delta y$ and every x with $x + \Delta x$.
Step 3: Work out right-hand side until there are no brackets left.
Step 4: Subtract the original terms, to be left with an equation in terms of Δy and Δx only.
Step 5: Divide across by Δx.
Step 6: Find $\displaystyle\lim_{\Delta x \to 0} \frac{\Delta y}{\Delta x}$ by replacing Δx by 0 everywhere it occurs.

Example: Differentiate $y = x^2 + 4x + 6$ from first principles.

Solution

$$y = x^2 + 4x + 6$$

replace x with Δx and y with Δy

$$y + \Delta y = (x + \Delta x)^2 + 4(x + \Delta x) + 6$$

multiply out right-hand side

$$y + \Delta y = x^2 + 2x\Delta x + \Delta x^2 + 4x + 4\Delta x + 6$$

subtract the original terms

$$y = x^2 + 4x + 6$$

$$\Delta y = 2x\Delta x + \Delta x^2 + 4\Delta x$$

divide across by Δx

$$\frac{\Delta y}{\Delta x} = 2x + \Delta x + 4$$

any Δx left becomes 0

$$\lim_{\Delta x \to 0} \frac{\Delta y}{\Delta x} = 2x + 4$$

Need to learn that:

$$(x + \Delta x)^2 = x^2 + 2x\Delta x + \Delta x^2$$

If you cannot learn it then it can be figured out.

squared means multiplied by itself

$(x + \Delta x)^2 = (x + \Delta x)(x + \Delta x)$

split the first bracket and write second one twice

$= x(x + \Delta x) + \Delta x(x + \Delta x)$

multiply out and add like terms

$= x^2 + x\Delta x + x\Delta x + \Delta x^2$

$= x^2 + 2x\Delta x + \Delta x^2$

Notation 2

Step 1: Let $f(x) =$ what we are given to differentiate in the question.
Step 2: To every x add h.
Step 3: Multiply out the right-hand side
Step 4: Subtract the original.
Step 5: Divide across by h.
Step 6: Anything with h goes to 0.

Example: Differentiate $f(x) = x^2 - 2x - 5$ from first principles.

Solution

$f(x) = x^2 - 2x - 5$

replace x with $x + h$

$f(x + h) = (x + h)^2 - 2(x + h) - 5$

multiply out

$f(x + h) = x^2 + 2xh + h^2 - 2x - 2h - 5$

subtract the original

$f(x) = x^2 - 2x - 5$

$f(x + h) - f(x) = 2xh + h^2 - 2h$

divide across by h

$\dfrac{f(x+h) - f(x)}{h} = 2x + h - 2$

let any h left become 0

$\lim\limits_{h \to 0} \dfrac{f(x+h) - f(x)}{h} = 2x - 2$

Need to learn that:

$(x + h)^2 = x^2 + 2xh + h^2$

If you cannot learn it then it can be figured out.

Squared means multiplied by itself

$(x + h)^2 = (x + h)(x + h)$

split the first bracket and write second one twice

$= x(x + h) + h(x + h)$

multiply out and add like terms

$= x^2 + xh + xh + h^2$

$= x^2 + 2xh + h^2$

Basic rules of differentiation

If $y = x^n$ then $\dfrac{dy}{dx} = nx^{n-1}$

Multiply by the power and reduce the power by one.

Say the rule over and over until it is second nature to you.

Do not forget your basic rules of indices and to use the maths tables when possible.

Example: Find $\dfrac{dy}{dx}$ if

(i) $y = 4x^2 + 3x + 6$
(ii) $y = 6x^4 - 2x^2$

Solution

(i) $y = 4x^2 + 3x + 6$

multiply by powers and reduce powers by one

$\dfrac{dy}{dx} = 8x + 3$

51

(ii) $y = 6x^4 - 2x^2$

multiply by powers and reduce powers by one

$$\frac{dy}{dx} = 24x^3 - 4x$$

Example: Find $\frac{dy}{dx}$ if $y = \frac{1}{x^2}$

Solution

$$y = \frac{1}{x^2}$$

use rules of indices $\frac{1}{a^n} = a^{-n}$

$$y = x^{-2}$$

now can use the rule multiply by power and reduce power by 1

$$\frac{dy}{dx} = -2x^{-3}$$

(one less than -2 is -3)
use the rules of indices to change back

$$a^{-n} = \frac{1}{a^n}$$

$$\frac{dy}{dx} = \frac{-2}{x^3}$$

Evaluating derivatives

Differentiate and sub in the given value.

Example: If $y = x^2 - 5x - 8$, find the value of x when $x = 3$.

Solution

$$y = x^2 - 5x - 8$$

multiply by power and reduce power by one

$$\frac{dy}{dx} = 2x - 5$$

sub in $x = 3$, replace every x with 3 and evaluate.

$$\frac{dy}{dx} = 2(3) - 5$$

$$= 6 - 5$$

$$= 1$$

Example: If $s = t^3 + 2t^2 - 5t$, find the value of $\frac{ds}{dt}$ when $t + 1 = 0$.

Solution

$$s = t^3 + 2t^2 - 5t$$

multiply by power and reduce power by one

$$\frac{ds}{dt} = 3t^2 + 4t - 5$$

if $t + 1 = 0 \Rightarrow t = -1$
sub in $t = -1$

$$\frac{ds}{dt} = 3(-1)^2 + 4(-1) - 5$$

$$= 3 - 4 - 5 = -6$$

Product rule

This can be harder to see, but is when we multiply two functions by each other.
If $y = u \cdot v$ then

$$\frac{dy}{dx} = u\frac{dv}{dx} + v\frac{du}{dx}$$

Note: Used when multiplying out two brackets with x in both.

Step 1: Let u = first bracket and v second bracket.

Step 2: Find $\dfrac{du}{dx}$ and $\dfrac{dv}{dx}$.

Step 3: Write down formula, which is on page 42 of the maths tables.

Step 4: Put result from steps 1 and 2 into formula and tidy up.

Example:
Differentiate $y = (2x - 3)(5x + 4)$.

Solution

$u = 2x - 3 \qquad v = 5x + 4$

$\dfrac{du}{dx} = 2 \qquad \dfrac{dv}{dx} = 5$

$\dfrac{dy}{dx} = u\dfrac{dv}{dx} + v\dfrac{du}{dx}$

$\dfrac{dy}{dx} = 5(2x - 3) + 2(5x + 4)$

$\qquad = 10x - 15 + 10x + 8$

$\qquad = 20x - 7$

Note: Make sure you do not get mixed up when writing down the letter u and the letter v.

Note: We should have written down $(2x - 3)5$, but it is easier to write down $5(2x - 3)$.

Note: An easy way out is to just multiply out the expression at the start and then differentiate:

$y = (2x - 3)(5x + 4)$

$y = 2x(5x + 4) - 3(5x + 4)$

$y = 10x^2 + 8x - 15x - 12$

$y = 10x^2 - 7x - 12$

$\dfrac{dy}{dx} = 20x - 7$

Quotient rule

This is used when we have division where there is an x on the bottom.

If $y = \dfrac{u}{v}$ then

$$\dfrac{dy}{dx} = \dfrac{v\dfrac{du}{dx} - u\dfrac{dv}{dx}}{v^2}$$

Step 1: Let u = top and v = bottom.

Step 2: Find $\dfrac{du}{dx}$ and $\dfrac{dv}{dx}$.

Step 3: Write down formula, which is on page 42 of the maths tables.

Step 4: Put result from steps 1 and 2 into formula and tidy up.

Example: If $y = \dfrac{3x - 5}{x - 2}$ find $\dfrac{dy}{dx}, x \neq 2$.

Solution

$u = 3x - 5 \qquad v = x - 2$

$\dfrac{du}{dx} = 3 \qquad \dfrac{dv}{dx} = 1$

$\dfrac{dy}{dx} = \dfrac{v\dfrac{du}{dx} - u\dfrac{dv}{dx}}{v^2}$

$\qquad = \dfrac{3(x - 2) - 1(3x - 5)}{(x - 2)^2}$

multiply out the top line and tidy up. Leave the bottom alone

$\qquad = \dfrac{3x - 6 - 3x + 5}{(x - 2)^2}$

$\qquad = \dfrac{-1}{(x - 2)^2}$

Chain rule

We use this when we have a power in the question.

This is done in two steps:

- Differentiate inside the brackets.
- Differentiate the power outside the bracket.

Example: Find $\frac{dy}{dx}$ when $y = (3x - 8)^4$.

Solution

$$y = (3x - 8)^4$$

differentiate inside and then the power outside.

$$\frac{dy}{dx} = 3(4)(3x - 8)^3$$

$$= 12(3x - 8)^3$$

Differentiate inside means $3x - 8$; when differentiated becomes 3.
Differentiate outside means $(3x - 8)^4$; when differentiated becomes $4(3x - 8)^3$.

Note: We can multiply the two parts that have no power on them: $3(4) = 12$

Example: Differentiate $y = (4x^3 - 5x^2 - 7)^7$ with respect to x.

Solution

$$y = (4x^3 - 5x^2 - 7)^7$$

$$\frac{dy}{dx} = (12x^2 - 10x)(7)(4x^3 - 5x^2 - 7)^6$$

$$= (84x^2 - 70x)(4x^3 - 5x^2 - 7)^6$$

Example: Given that $y = (x^2 - 2x + 2)^3$, show that $\frac{dy}{dx} = 0$ when $x = 1$.

Solution

$$y = (x^2 - 2x + 2)^3$$

$$\frac{dy}{dx} = (2x - 2)(3)(x^2 - 2x + 2)^2$$

$$= (6x - 6)(x^2 - 2x + 2)^2$$

sub in $x = 1$, replace every x with 1 and evaluate

$$y = (6(1) - 6)((1)^2 - 2(1) + 2)^2$$

$$= (6 - 6)(1 - 2 + 2)^2$$

$$= (0)(1)^2 = 0$$

To find the slope and equation of a tangent to a curve at a point on the curve

A tangent is a *line* that hits a curve at one point only.

Since it is a line then we need:

- a point
- the slope.

Once we have the point and slope we can use the formula for equation of a line, $y - y_1 = m(x - x_1)$, to find the equation of the tangent.

$$m = \frac{dy}{dx} = \text{Slope of tangent at the point } (x, y)$$

Note: There are other ways of finding the slope of a curve:

(a) Slope between two points

$$m = \frac{y_2 - y_1}{x_2 - x_1}.$$

(b) Slope of the line $ax + by + c = 0$ is

$$m = -\frac{a}{b}.$$

Example: Find the equation of the tangent to the curve $y = x^3 - 4x^2 + x + 2$ at the point $(1, 0)$.

Solution

Have the point but not the slope:

> Differentiate to find the slope at any point along the line.
> Sub in the x value from the point we were given to find the slope at that point given.
> Use the equation $y - y_1 = m(x - x_1)$ to find our answer.

$$y = x^3 - 4x^2 + x + 2$$

$$\frac{dy}{dx} = 3x^2 - 8x + 1$$

sub in $x = 1$ into $\frac{dy}{dx}$ to find the value of the slope

$$m = 3(1)^2 - 8(1) + 1$$
$$= 3 - 8 + 1$$
$$= -4$$

equation of tangent $y - y_1 = m(x - x_1)$ with point $(1, 0)$ from question, and slope $m = -4$ that we have found through differentiation

$$y - 0 = -4(x - 1)$$
$$y = -4x + 4$$
$$4x + y = 4$$

Example: Find the point on the curve $y = x^2 + 3x - 2$ where the tangents are parallel to the line $5x - y = 4$.

Solution

$$m = \frac{dy}{dx} = 2x + 3$$

Slope of $5x - y = 4$ is $m = \frac{-5}{-1} = 5$.

Note: Parallel means that the slopes are the same.

$$2x + 3 = 5$$

let the slopes be equal and solve the equation

$$2x = 2$$
$$x = 1$$

> **Note:** To find the value of y, sub the value of x into the original.

Sub $x = 1$ into $y = x^2 + 3x - 2$ to get $y = 2$. The point is $(1, 2)$.

Example: Let $f(x) = \frac{1}{x - 1}, x \in R, x \neq 1$.

(i) Find $f'(x)$, the derivative of $f(x)$.
(ii) There are two points on the curve $f(x)$ at which the slope of the tangent is perpendicular to $4x - y = 7$. Find the coordinates of these two points.

Note: $f'(x) = \frac{dy}{dx}$

Solution

$f(x) = \frac{1}{x - 1}$ to differentiate we must use the quotient rule

$u = 1$ $v = x - 1$

$\frac{du}{dx} = 0$ $\frac{dv}{dx} = 1$

$$\frac{dy}{dx} = \frac{v\frac{du}{dx} - u\frac{dv}{dx}}{v^2}$$

55

$$= \frac{0(x-1) - 1(1)}{(x-1)^2}$$

multiply out the top line and tidy up. Leave the bottom alone.

$$= \frac{-1}{(x-1)^2}$$

Note: $0(x-1) = 0$, as 0 by anything equals 0.

Note: Perpendicular means turn the slope upside down and change the sign.

Slope of $4x - y = 7$ is $m = \frac{-4}{-1} = 4$

Required slope $m = -\frac{1}{4}$

(upside down and change the sign)

$m = -\frac{1}{4}$.

We have differentiated and found

$\frac{dy}{dx} = \frac{-1}{(x-1)^2}$, so $m = \frac{-1}{(x-1)^2}$.

Let the two slopes be equal and solve the equation using algebra

$$\frac{-1}{(x-1)^2} = -\frac{1}{4}$$

get a common denominator or cross-multiply

$$\frac{-4 = -(x-1)^2}{4(x-1)^2}$$

drop the bottom

$$-4 = -(x-1)^2$$

change the sign of both sides; squared means multiplied by itself

$$4 = (x-1)(x-1)$$
$$4 = x(x-1) - 1(x-1)$$

multiply out the right-hand side

$$4 = x^2 - x - x + 1$$

bring all the terms to the left

$$4 - x^2 + 2x - 1 = 0$$

tidy up

$$3 - x^2 + 2x = 0$$

change the sign of the whole line

$$x^2 - 2x - 3 = 0$$

solve the quadratic

$$(x-3)(x+1) = 0$$
$$x = 3 \text{ or } x = -1$$

Note: You must remember with questions like these that they are (c)-type questions. The more you can do, the more marks you will pick up. You do not have to get the whole lot done. You need to put some time and effort into algebra to take the fear out of it.

Example: Let $f(x) = x^3 + 2ax + 8$ for all $x \in R$ and for $a \in R$.
The slope of the tangent to the curve $y = f(x)$ at $x = 2$ is 14. Find the value of a.

Solution

$$y = x^3 + 2ax + 8$$
$$\frac{dy}{dx} = 3x^2 + 2a$$

To find the slope sub $x = 2$ into $\frac{dy}{dx}$ and let the answer = 14, since we are told this in the question.

$$3(2)^2 + 2a = 14$$
$$12 + 2a = 14$$
$$2a = 2$$
$$a = 1$$

To find the maximum and minimum points of a curve

Stationary points are the same as turning points, which means the same as max or min points.
$$\frac{dy}{dx} = 0$$

(i) Maximum $\frac{dy}{dx} = 0$ and $\frac{d^2y}{dx^2} < 0$.

(ii) Minimum $\frac{dy}{dx} = 0$ and $\frac{d^2y}{dx^2} > 0$.

Step 1: Find $\frac{dy}{dx}$.

Step 2: Let $\frac{dy}{dx} = 0$ and solve the equation formed.

Step 3: Substitute the values of x in the above into the *original* to get y.

Step 4: Differentiate twice to get $\frac{d^2y}{dx^2}$ and sub in the x value to determine if it is a max or a min.

Example: Find the coordinates of the maximum point and the coordinates of the minimum point of the curve $y = x^3 - 3x - 4$.

Solution

Step 1: Must first find $\frac{dy}{dx}$.

$$y = x^3 - 3x - 4$$
$$\frac{dy}{dx} = 3x^2 - 3$$

Step 2: Let $\frac{dy}{dx} = 0$ and solve the equation formed.

$$3x^2 - 3 = 0$$

divide across by 3
$$x^2 - 1 = 0$$

factorise the quadratic using the difference of 2 squares
$$(x - 1)(x + 1) = 0$$

let each factor equal 0

$x - 1 = 0$ $\qquad$ $x + 1 = 0$

or

$x = 1$ $\qquad$ $x = -1$

Step 3: Substitute the values of x in the above into the *original* to get y.

When $x = 1$
$$y = 1^3 - 3(1) - 4 = -6$$

One point is $(1, -6)$

When $x = -1$
$$y = (-1)^3 - 3(-1) - 4 = -2$$

Other point is $(-1, -2)$

Note: Every point is written as (x, y).

Step 4: Differentiate twice and sub in the x value to determine if it is a max or a min.

$$y = x^3 - 3x - 4$$
$$\frac{dy}{dx} = 3x^2 - 3$$
$$\frac{d^2y}{dx^2} = 6x$$

57

When $x = 1$

$$\frac{d^2y}{dx^2} = 6(1) = 6 > 0,$$

so this is the minimum point by the rules given above.

When $x = -1$

$$\frac{d^2y}{dx^2} = 6(-1) = -6 < 0,$$

so this is the maximum point by the rules given above.

Example: Let $f(x) = x^2 + ax + 4$ for all $x \in R$ and for $a \in R$.

$f(x)$ has a turning point at $x = 3$. Find the value of a.

Solution

$$f(x) = x^2 + ax + 4$$
$$f'(x) = 2x + a$$

sub in $x = 3$ and let $f'(x) = 0$, since it is a turning point

$$2(3) + a = 0$$
$$6 + a = 0$$
$$a = -6$$

Quadratic graphs

Example: Let $f(x) = x^2 - 2x - 8$, $x \in R$.

(i) Find $f'(x)$, the derivative of $f(x)$, and hence find the coordinates of the local minimum point of the curve $y = f(x)$.
(ii) Solve the equation $f(x) = 0$.
(iii) Use your answers from parts (i) and (ii) to sketch the graph of the curve $y = f(x)$.

Solution

(i) $\quad f(x) = x^2 - 2x - 8$

$$f'(x) = \frac{dy}{dx} = 2x - 2$$

for max or min let $f'(x) = \frac{dy}{dx} = 0$.

$$2x - 2 = 0$$
$$2x = 2$$
$$x = 1$$
$$f(1) = 1^2 - 2(1) - 8$$
$$= 1 - 2 - 8 = -9$$

Point is $(1, -9)$

(ii) $\quad f(x) = 0$

sub in the equation and solve the quadratic equation

$$x^2 - 2x - 8 = 0$$
$$(x - 4)(x + 2) = 0$$

$x - 4 = 0 \qquad x + 2 = 0$

or

$x = 4 \qquad x = -2$

Points are $(4, 0)$ and $(-2, 0)$

We now have 3 points $(1, -9)$, $(4, 0)$ and $(-2, 0)$, which we can show on a diagram and join freehand.

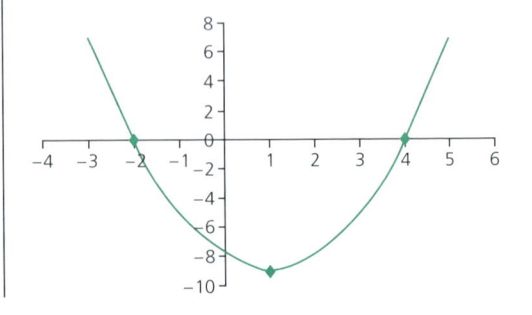

Cubic graphs

Example: Let $f(x) = x^3 - 3x^2 + 6$, $x \in R$.

(i) Find $f(-1)$ and $f(3)$.
(ii) Find $f'(x)$, the derivative of $f(x)$.
(iii) Find the coordinates of the local maximum point and the local minimum point of the curve $y = f(x)$.
(iv) Draw a graph of the function f in the domain $-1 \leq x \leq 3$.

Solution

(i) $f(x) = x^3 - 3x^2 + 6$

sub in $x = -1$

$$f(-1) = (-1)^3 - 3(-1)^2 + 6$$
$$= -1 - 3(1) + 6$$
$$= -1 - 3 + 6 = 2$$

Point is $(-1, 2)$

sub in $x = 3$

$$f(3) = 3^3 - 3(3)^2 + 6$$
$$= 27 - 3(9) + 6$$
$$= 27 - 27 + 6 = 6$$

Point is $(3, 6)$

(ii) $f'(x) = \dfrac{dy}{dx} = 3x^2 - 6x$

(iii) For max or min $\dfrac{dy}{dx} = 0$, so

$3x^2 - 6x = 0$ divide across by 3
$x^2 - 2x = 0$ take out what's common
$x(x - 2) = 0$
$x = 0$ or $x = 2$

Put the values of x back into the original:
sub $x = 0$ into $f(x) = x^3 - 3x^2 + 6$,
so $y = 6$
One turning point is $(0, 6)$.

Sub $x = 0$ into $y = x^3 - 3x^2 + 6$,
so $y = 2$
Other turning point is $(2, 2)$.

This time we have 4 points $(-1, 2)$, $(0, 6)$, $(2, 2)$ and $(3, 6)$, which we can plot on a diagram and join freehand.

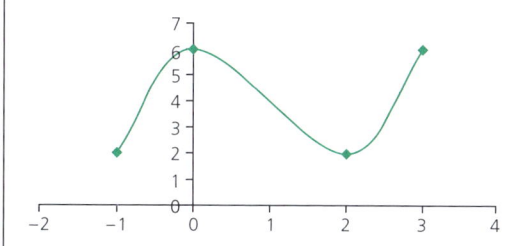

Fraction graphs

Example: Let $f(x) = \dfrac{1}{x - 2}$ where $x \in R$ and $x \neq 2$.

(i) Find the value of $f(-1), f(0), f(3)$ and $f(4)$.
(ii) For what real value of x is $f(x)$ not defined?
(iii) Find $f'(x)$, the derivative of $f(x)$.
(iv) Draw a graph of $f(x) = \dfrac{1}{x - 2}$ for $-1 \leq x \leq 5$.

Solution

(i) $\quad f(-1) = \dfrac{1}{-1 - 2} = -\dfrac{1}{3}$

Point is $\left(-1, -\dfrac{1}{3}\right)$

$\quad f(0) = \dfrac{1}{0 - 2} = -\dfrac{1}{2}$

Point is $\left(0, -\dfrac{1}{2}\right)$

$\quad f(3) = \dfrac{1}{3 - 2} = 1$

Point is $(3, 1)$

59

$$f(4) = \frac{1}{4-2} = \frac{1}{2}$$

Point is $\left(4, \frac{1}{2}\right)$

(ii) $\boxed{f(x) \text{ not defined means that the bottom} = 0.}$

$$x - 2 = 0$$
$$x = 2$$

(iii) $f(x) = \frac{1}{x-2}$ to differentiate we must use the quotient rule

$u = 1$ $v = x - 2$

$\frac{du}{dx} = 0$ $\frac{dv}{dx} = 1$

$$\frac{dy}{dx} = \frac{v\frac{du}{dx} - u\frac{dv}{dx}}{v^2}$$

$$= \frac{0(x-2) - 1(1)}{(x-2)^2}$$

multiply out the top line and tidy up. Leave the bottom alone

$$= \frac{-1}{(x-2)^2}$$

(iv) To draw a diagram.

This time we have 4 points

$\left(-1, -\frac{1}{3}\right), \left(0, -\frac{1}{2}\right), \left(1, -\frac{1}{3}\right)$, and $\left(4, \frac{1}{2}\right)$ which we can plot on a diagram.

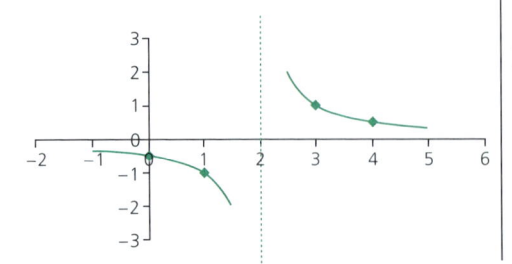

We can join (freehand) only the points on either side of the axis and on either side of the line $x = 2$. If you do not put in the line $x = 2$ you will not lose marks, but it is harder to draw the diagram.

Speed and acceleration

If we are given distance (s) as a function of time (t), then:

- speed or velocity = $\frac{ds}{dt}$, the rate of change of distance with respect to time.

- acceleration = $\frac{d^2s}{dt^2}$, the rate of change of speed with respect to time.

Example: If the distance s metres travelled by a body in t seconds is given by $s = 10t + 2t^2 + t^3$, find:

(i) the distance travelled after 5 seconds
(ii) the velocity (speed) of the body after 10 seconds
(iii) the acceleration of the body after 6 seconds.

Solution

(i) If asked to find the distance, just put the given time into the given equation.

Distance $s = 10(5) + 2(5)^2 + 5^3$ sub in $t = 5$

$$= 50 + 50 + 125$$
$$= 225 \text{ metres}$$

(ii) If asked to find velocity, differentiate once and then sub in the given time.

Distance $s = 10t + 2t^2 + t^3$

Speed $\dfrac{ds}{dt} = 10 + 4t + 3t^2$ sub in $t = 10$

$= 10 + 4(10) + 3(10)^2$

$= 10 + 40 + 300 = 350$ m/s

(iii) If asked to find acceleration, differentiate twice and then sub in the given time.

Distance $s = 10t + 2t^2 + t^3$

Speed $\dfrac{ds}{dt} = 10 + 4t + 3t^2$

Acceleration $\dfrac{d^2s}{dt^2} = 4 + 6t$ sub in $t = 6$

$= 4 + 6(6) = 40$ m/s^2

Example: A rocket is fired up in the air. The height s reached by the rocket after t seconds is given by $s = 12t - t^2$. Find:

(a) the speed of the rocket when it is fired
(b) the time taken to reach the maximum height
(c) the maximum height reached
(d) the acceleration of the rocket.

Solution

(a) To find the speed of the rocket when it is fired means we differentiate and sub in $t = 0$.

Height $s = 12t - t^2$

Speed $\dfrac{ds}{dt} = 12 - 2t$ sub in $t = 0$

$\dfrac{ds}{dt} = 12$ m/s

(b) To find time to maximum height differentiate and let $= 0$.

$s = 12t - t^2$

$\dfrac{ds}{dt} = 12 - 2t = 0$

$2t = 12$

$t = 6$

(c) To find the maximum height reached sub $t = 6$ into $s = 12t - t^2$.

$s = 12(6) - 6^2$

$= 36$ m

(d) To find the acceleration of the rocket, differentiate twice.

$s = 12t - t^2$

Speed $\dfrac{ds}{dt} = 12 - 2t$

Acceleration $\dfrac{d^2s}{dt^2} = -2$ m/s^2

Example: The volume V of a certain gas is given by $V = \dfrac{600}{p}$, where p is the pressure. Find the rate of change of V with respect to p when $p = 20$.

Solution

Differentiate first (that is what rate of change means) and then sub in the given value. If in doubt, differentiate in Q6, Q7 or Q8 on Paper I.

Use the quotient rule.

$u = 600 \qquad v = p$

$\dfrac{du}{dx} = 0 \qquad \dfrac{dv}{dp} = 1$

$\dfrac{dV}{dp} = \dfrac{p(0) - 600(1)}{p^2}$

$\dfrac{dV}{dp} = \dfrac{-600}{p^2}$ sub in $p = 20$

$\dfrac{dV}{dp} = \dfrac{-600}{20^2} = \dfrac{-600}{400} = -\dfrac{3}{2}$

Chapter 6
Functions and Graphs

Contents

(a) Functions (page 62)
(b) Graphs (page 66)
(c) Period and range (page 67).

Functions

> Function means that our answer depends on the value of x we put through a given rule.

x is called the input value, which we put through the given rule to get our output value $f(x)$. Sometimes it is easier to call $f(x) = y$ so that we can put the couple together and show the input and output values together on a graph.

Note: $f(x) = g(x) = h(x)$; all are the same, just different letters.

Example: If $f(x) = 3x - 2$, find $f(4)$.

Solution
This is an easy one to start us off but we will do the same process over and over again in all the examples that follow.
 We are given the rule $3x - 2$. We put in $x = 4$ to see what our answer is.

$f(4) = 3(4) - 2$ replace the x with 4

$\quad\quad = 12 - 2 = 10$ multiply first then add and subtract

Example: If $f(x) = 3x^2 - 5x$ find:

(i) $f(3)$
(ii) $f(-2)$

Solution

(i)   replace the x with 3

$\quad\quad f(3) = 3(3)^2 - 5(3)$

square first then multiply

$\quad\quad\quad = 3(9) - 15$

$\quad\quad\quad = 27 - 15 = 12$

(ii)   replace first x with -2

$\quad\quad f(-2) = 3(-2)^2 - 5(-2)$

square first then multiply

$\quad\quad\quad = 3(4) + 10$

$\quad\quad\quad = 12 + 10 = 22$

Example: Let $g(x) = \dfrac{1}{2x - 1}$. Evaluate $g(3)$.

Solution

$g(x) = \dfrac{1}{2x - 1}$ sub in $x = 3$

$g(3) = \dfrac{1}{2(3) - 1}$ tidy up the bottom

$\quad\quad = \dfrac{1}{6 - 1} = \dfrac{1}{5}$

can leave the answer as a fraction.

Example: Given that $h(x) = x^2$, write down $h(x + 3)$.

Hence, find the values of x for which $h(x) = h(x + 3)$.

Solution

$$h(x) = x^2$$

replace the x with $x + 3$

$$h(x + 3) = (x + 3)^2$$

Note: Getting this far will pick you up marks even if you cannot finish the question off.

$$h(x) = h(x + 3)$$
$$x^2 = (x + 3)^2$$

square means multiply by itself

$$x^2 = (x + 3)(x + 3)$$

split the brackets and multiply out

$$x^2 = x(x + 3) + 3(x + 3)$$
$$x^2 = x^2 + 3x + 3x + 9$$

cancel the x^2 from both sides and solve the equation

$$0 = 6x + 9$$
$$-6x = 9$$
$$6x = -9$$
$$x = -\frac{9}{6} = -\frac{3}{2}$$

Example: Given $g(x) = x^2$ and $h(x) = 2x + 3$, find the values of x for which $g(x) = h(x)$.

Solution

Follow what you are given. $g(x) = h(x)$, so replace $g(x)$ with x^2 and $h(x)$ with $2x + 3$ and solve the quadratic equation.

$$g(x) = h(x)$$
$$x^2 = 2x + 3$$
$$x^2 - 2x - 3 = 0$$
$$(x - 3)(x + 1) = 0$$
$$x - 3 = 0 \quad\quad x + 1 = 0$$
$$\text{or}$$
$$x = 3 \quad\quad x = -1$$

One Unknown

Example: Given $f(x) = 3x - 2$, find k if $f(k) = 19$.

Solution

The method does not change.

$$f(x) = 3x - 2$$

sub in $x = k$ and let the answer $= 19$

$$f(k) = 3k - 2 = 19$$
$$3k = 21$$

solve the simple equation

$$k = 7$$

Example: If $g(x) = 2x - 5$, find k if $g(k + 1) = 19$.

Solution

$$g(x) = 2x - 5$$

sub in $x = k + 1$ and let the answer $= 19$

$$g(k + 1) = 2(k + 1) - 5 = 19$$
$$2k + 2 - 5 = 19$$
$$2k - 3 = 19$$
$$2k = 22$$
$$k = 11$$

Example: If $f(x) = 4x + b$, find the value of b given that $f(2) = 11$.

Solution
$$f(x) = 4x + b$$
Sub in $x = 2$ and let answer $= 11$
$$f(2) = 4(2) + b = 11$$
$$8 + b = 11$$
$$b = 3$$

Example: Given that $g(x) = ax + 5$, find the value of a given that $g(2) = -9$.
$$g(x) = ax + 5$$

Solution
Sub in $x = 2$ and let answer $= -9$
$$g(2) = 2a + 5 = -9$$
$$2a = -14$$
$$a = -7$$

Example: If $f(x) = 2x - 9$, find the value of k if $f(0) = k[f(3)]$.

Solution
Need to find $f(0)$ and $f(3)$ and then form an equation to find k.
$$f(x) = 2x - 9$$
$$f(0) = 2(0) - 9$$
$$= 0 - 9 = -9$$
$$f(x) = 2x - 9$$
$$f(3) = 2(3) - 9$$
$$= 6 - 9 = -3$$
$$f(0) = k[f(3)]$$
substitute $f(0) = -9$ and $f(3) = -3$
$$-9 = -3k$$
change sign of both sides
$$9 = 3k$$
swap both sides so that letters on left and numbers on right
$$3k = 9$$
$$k = 3$$

Two Unknowns

When there are two unknowns the solution will nearly always involve solving simultaneous equations from algebra.

Example: If $f(x) = ax + b$ find the value of a and b, given that $f(2) = 7$ and $f(3) = 13$

Solution
$$f(x) = ax + b$$
$$f(2) = 2a + b = 7$$
$$f(3) = 3a + b = 13$$
Use simultaneous equations to find $a = 6$ and $b = -5$.

Example: $f(x) = ax^2 + bx - 8$, where a and b are real numbers.

If $f(1) = -9$ and $f(-1) = 3$, find the value of a and the value of b.

Solution
$$f(x) = ax^2 + bx - 8$$
sub in $x = 1$ and let answer $= -9$
$$f(1) = a(1)^2 + b(1) - 8 = -9$$
$$a + b - 8 = -9$$
$$a + b = -1$$

Note: It is very important here and for

drawing graphs that you always square (or cube) the number first, then multiply.

$$f(x) = ax^2 + bx - 8$$

sub in $x = -1$ and let answer = 3

$$f(-1) = a(-1)^2 + b(-1) - 8 = 3$$
$$a(1) - b - 8 = 3$$
$$a - b = 11$$

Use simultaneous equations:

$$a + b = -1$$
$$a - b = 11$$

Answers are $a = 5$ and $b = -6$.

Example: If $g(x) = 2x^2 + ax + b$, find the value of a and the value of b.

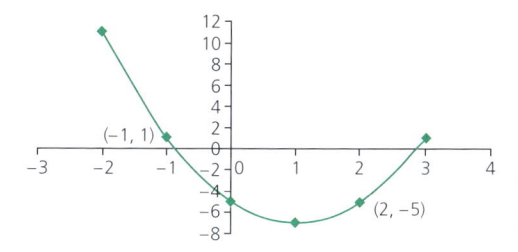

Solution

From the diagram we know two points are $(-1, 1)$ and $(2, -5)$. What use can we make of this?

$(-1, 1)$ means when $x = -1$, then $y = g(x) = 1$

$$g(x) = 2x^2 + ax + b$$
$$g(-1) = 2(-1)^2 + a(-1) + b = 1$$
$$2 - a + b = 1$$
$$-a + b = -1$$
$$a - b = 1$$

$(2, -5)$ means when $x = 2$, then $y = g(x) = -5$

$$g(x) = 2x^2 + ax + b$$
$$g(2) = 2(2)^2 + a(2) + b = -5$$
$$8 + 2a + b = -5$$
$$2a + b = -13$$

Use simultaneous equations to find answers of $a = -4$ and $b = -5$.

Example: The curve $f(x) = x^2 - 2x - 3$ is as shown. Find the points p, q and r.

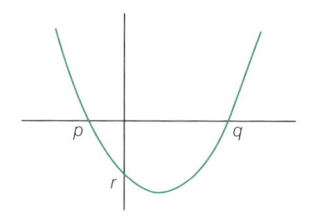

Solution

The curve $f(x) = x^2 - 2x - 3$ can be written $y = x^2 - 2x - 3$.

The points p and q are where the graph cuts the x-axis. On the x-axis, $y = 0$.

Let $x^2 - 2x - 3 = 0$ and solve the quadratic.

$$x^2 - 3x + x - 3 = 0$$
$$x(x - 3) + 1(x - 3) = 0$$
$$(x - 3)(x + 1) = 0$$
$$x - 3 = 0 \qquad x + 1 = 0$$
or
$$x = 3 \qquad x = -1$$

p is the point $(-1, 0)$ and q is the point $(3, 0)$

The point r is where the curve cuts the y-axis, so $x = 0$.

$$y = (0)^2 - 2(0) - 3 = -3$$

r is the point $(0, -3)$.

65

Graphs

There are 3 general types of graph that they can ask us to draw.

Note: All diagrams are drawn on graph paper using a pencil.

Graph 1: Graph of two lines

Example: Using the same axes, draw the graphs of $x + 2y = 6$ and $x - 2y = 2$. Find their point of intersection using simultaneous equations.

This is especially important in linear programming.

To find where a line cuts the x-axis, put $y = 0$ into the equation and get a value for x.
To find where a line cuts the y-axis, put $x = 0$ into the equation and get a value for y.

Solution
Draw the line $x + 2y = 6$.
 Find where it cuts the x-axis, so sub in $y = 0$ to get $x = 6$. One point is $(6, 0)$.
 Find where it cuts the y-axis, so sub in $x = 0$ to get $2y = 6$ ∴ $y = 3$. One point is $(0, 3)$.

Draw the line $x - 2y = 2$.
 Find where it cuts the x-axis, so sub in $y = 0$ to get $x = 2$. One point is $(2, 0)$.
 Find where it cuts the y-axis, so sub in $x = 0$ to get $-2y = 2$ ∴ $y = -1$. One point is $(0, -1)$.

Note: The points on the lines are joined using a ruler.

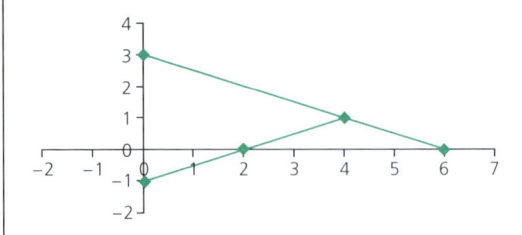

We can see the point of intersection is $(4, 1)$, but we must use simultaneous equations to verify this, since it is asked in the question.

$x + 2y = 6$
$x - 2y = 2$ the signs in front of the
─────── y are different, so add
              all the terms
$2x = 8$ divide across by the
              number in front of the
              x to get
$x = 4$

Put $x = 4$ back into the top equation

$4 + 2y = 6$
$2y = 2$
$y = 1$

The answer is $(4, 1)$.

Graph 2: Graph of quadratics

Example: Draw the graph of $f(x) = 2x^2 - 2x - 3$ in the domain $-2 \leq x \leq 3$, $x \in R$.

Solution
'In the domain $-2 \leq x \leq 3$' means we take values of x as $-2, -1, 0, 1, 2, 3$ and form a table.

66

x	−2	−1	0	1	2	3
$2x^2$	8	2	0	2	8	18
$-2x$	4	2	0	−2	−4	−6
−3	−3	−3	−3	−3	−3	−3
y	9	1	−3	−3	1	9

Couple the points together into (−2, 9), (−1, 1), (0, −3), (1, −3), (2, 1) and (3, 9)

Note: Each line in the table is different.

$2x^2$ means we put in each value of x: **square it first and then multiply** by 2.

$-2x$ means we put in each value of x and multiply by −2

−3 goes the whole way along as it has no x.

Remember two main things here:

(i) Square first then multiply.
(ii) Any number squared is positive.

Note: Show the points on graph paper and join the dots freehand.

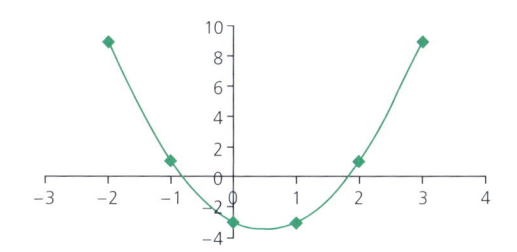

Graph 3: Graph of cubic equations

Example: Draw the graph of
$f(x) = x^3 - 2x^2 - 2x + 3$
in the domain $-2 \leq x \leq 3, x \in R$.

Solution

x	−2	−1	0	1	2	3
x^3	−8	−1	0	1	8	27
$-2x^2$	−8	−2	0	−2	−8	−18
$-2x$	4	2	0	−2	−4	−6
3	3	3	3	3	3	3
y	−9	2	3	0	−1	6

Couple the points together as (−2, −9), (−1, 2), (0, 3), (1, 0), (2, −1) and (3, 6)

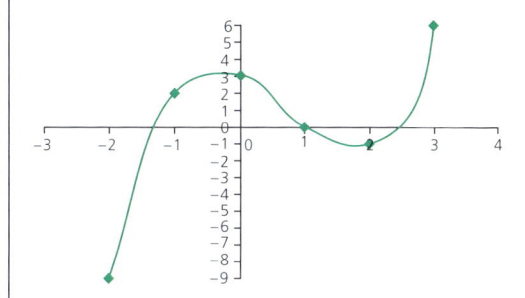

Note: Each line in the table is different.

x^3 means take the number and cube it.

$-2x^2$ means we put in each value of x: **square it first and then multiply** by −2.

$-2x$ means we put in each value of x and multiply by −2

3 goes the whole way along as it has no x.

Period and range

Period: This is how quickly the graph repeats.

Range: This is from how low the graph goes to how high it goes: lowest y-value to highest y-value.

Example: Part of the graph of a periodic function $f(x)$ is as shown.

(i) Write down the period and range.

(ii) Use the graph to find the value of $f(12)$ and $f(17)$.

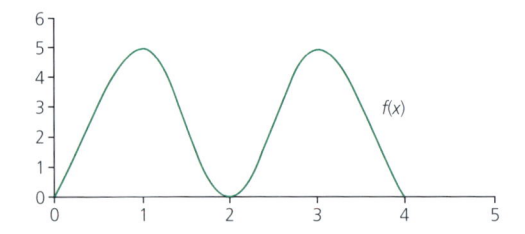

Solution

Period: This is how quickly the graph repeats; in this case, how long did it take the pattern to start all over again? Answer = 2

Range is from the lowest point to the highest point: Answer 0 to 5 = 5.

To find $f(12)$: we already know that after every 2 spaces the graph repeats, so that
$f(2) = f(4) = f(6) = f(8) = f(10) = f(12)$
(we do not have to write this out; just figure it out). This means the value of y when $x = 12$ is the same as the value of y when $x = 0$. $f(12) = 0$

$f(17) = f(1) = 5$, since $f(1) = f(3) = f(5)$ $= f(7) = f(9) = f(11) = f(13) = f(15)$ $= f(17)$ since period is 2.

Chapter 7
Area and Volume

Contents:

(i) Area and perimeter (page 69)
(ii) Volume and area of a box (page 73)
(iii) Volume and area of a cylinder (page 73)
(iv) Volume and area of a sphere and hemisphere (page 75)
(v) Volume and area of a cone (page 75).
(vi) Volume of triangular prism or wedge (page 76)
(vii) Melt down and recast (page 76)
(viii) Water displacement (page 77)
(ix) Rate of flow of liquid (page 78)
(x) Shape within a shape (page 78)
(xi) Double shapes (page 79)
(xii) Simpson's Rule (page 82).

Area and perimeter

Basic shapes

There are a number of different shapes we have to deal with:

(i) squares or rectangles
(ii) circles or parts of circles
(iii) triangles and parallelograms
(iv) double shapes.

When doing any of the questions on area and volume it is a good idea to use the following steps:

> ➢ Write out the information in the question, i.e. radius, height, length and so on.
> ➢ Write down a formula.
> ➢ Try to put the figures from the question into the formula to give you an answer.

Note: If it will help to make it clear, then draw a diagram.

> The most important thing to remember is that the answer is in the question, so use your eyes and use the right formula. Some of the formulae are in the maths tables, but others of them must be learnt off.

Square or rectangles (learn formulae)

A rectangle has two sets of equal sides:

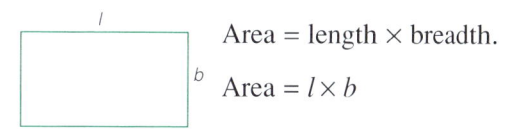

Area = length × breadth.
Area = $l \times b$

Perimeter = 2(length + breadth).
Perimeter = $2(l \times b)$

69

Triangles and parallelograms (learn formulae)

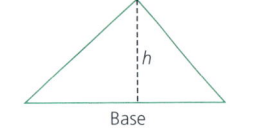

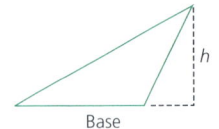

Area of triangle = half base by perpendicular height

Area of parallelogram = base by perpendicular height

Circles

Notes
(i) All the formulae here deal with the radius, so always try to write down what the radius is.
(ii) Remember the diameter is twice the radius: $d = 2r$
(iii) All the following formulae are on pages 6 and 7 of the maths tables.
(iv) All the formulae contain π. In the questions we are going to do, π can be written in 3 different ways:
 (a) $\pi = \pi$. We use this when we are asked to write the answer in terms of π.
 (b) $\pi = 3.14$
 (c) $\pi = \frac{22}{7}$

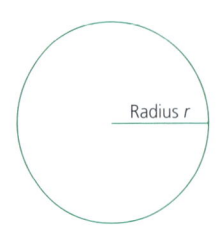

Circumference = $2\pi r$
Area = πr^2

(v) Be careful of the word 'circumference', which is the distance around the outside of a circle, because the maths tables and a lot of questions use the word 'length' or even 'perimeter'.
(vi) When you look up the formula for the area of a circle in the maths tables they call the circle a 'disc'.

Example: A rectangle of area 60 cm has a length of 18 cm. Find its width.

Solution

This is a very easy question to start with but you must get into good habits early, so follow the method outlined above no matter how easy or how hard the question may appear.

Rectangle: $l = 18$, $A = 60$; find b

Area = $l \times b$

$60 = 18l$ swap sides

$18l = 60$ divide by 18

$l = \frac{60}{18} = 3\frac{1}{3}$ cm

Note: Answers do not always have to be nice whole numbers!

Example: Find the area and circumference of a circle of diameter 4 m, when $\pi = 3.14$.

Solution

Circle: $r = 2$, $\pi = 3.14$; find A

Area = πr^2

= $3.14(2^2)$

square first, then multiply

= $3.14(4) = 12.56$

circumference = length = $2\pi r$

$2(3.14)(2) = 12.56$ m

Example: A circle has an area of 200.96 m². Find its radius.

Solution

Circle: $A = 200.96$, $\pi = 3.14$; find r.

Area = πr^2

$200.96 = 3.14r^2$ swap both sides

$3.14r^2 = 200.96$ divide by 3.14

$r^2 = \dfrac{200.96}{3.14}$

$r^2 = 64$

to get rid of square, find the square root

$r = 8$ m²

Sector of a circle

Make a fraction by using: $\dfrac{\text{Given angle}}{360}$

Example: Find the area and perimeter of the sector below to 1 decimal place when $\pi = \dfrac{22}{7}$.

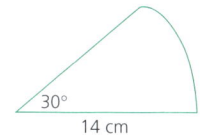

30°
14 cm

Solution

Find the area of a full circle, and then decide what fraction of a circle we have.

Circle: $r = 14$, $\pi = \dfrac{22}{7}$; find A

Area = πr^2

$= \dfrac{22}{7}(14)^2$

$= \dfrac{22}{7}\left(\dfrac{14}{1}\right)\left(\dfrac{14}{1}\right)$

divide 7 on bottom into 14 on top

$= 22(2)(14) = 616$

$30° = \dfrac{30}{360} = \dfrac{1}{12}$

(on a calculator put in 30 $\boxed{a^b/c}$ 360 = and it will give 1 r 12)

Answer $\dfrac{616}{12} = 51.3$ cm²

To find the length of the curved part (arc) find the circumference of a full circle and divide by 12.

Length = $2\pi r$

$= 2\left(\dfrac{22}{7}\right)\left(\dfrac{14}{1}\right)$ divide 7 into 14

$= 2(22)(2) = 88$

Arc length = $\dfrac{88}{12} = 7.3$ cm

Note: Perimeter is the total distance around the outside, which consists of 2 straight lengths and the arc length.

Perimeter = $14 + 14 + 7.3 = 35.3$

Note: If you do not like using $\pi = \dfrac{22}{7}$ you can use $\pi = 3.14$, but you may lose marks in the exam.

Double shapes

Most shapes are made up of parts of circles and rectangles, so take your time and try to use the correct formula.

Example: Find the shaded region if the radius of the circle is 12 m, when $\pi = 3.14$.

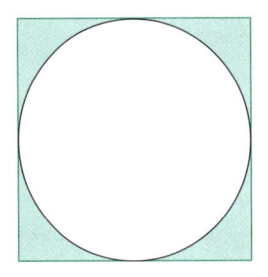

Write down the shapes you see, then deal with each shape on its own.

Solution

Shaded area = Area of square – area of circle.

Square: $l = 24$ and $b = 24$, since radius of the circle is 12; therefore the diameter is 24.

$$\text{Area} = l \times b$$
$$= 24 \times 24 = 576$$

Circle: $r = 12$ and $\pi = 3.14$; find A

$$\text{Area} = \pi r^2$$
$$= 3.14(12)^2$$
$$= 3.14(144)$$
$$= 452.16$$

Shaded area = $576 - 452.16 = 123.84$ m².

Example: Find the shaded region if the radius of the circle is 7 m, when $\pi = \frac{22}{7}$.

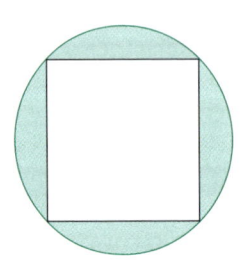

Solution

Shaded area = Area of circle – area of square.

Circle: $r = 7$ and $\pi = \frac{22}{7}$

$$\text{Area} = \pi r^2$$
$$= \frac{22}{7}(7)^2$$
$$= \frac{22}{7}\left(\frac{7}{1}\right)\left(\frac{7}{1}\right)$$
$$= 22(7) = 154 \text{ m}^2$$

Take the square and draw a diagonal $[cb]$ across it. Draw a line from the centre to the other corner. These lines must be at right angles to each other, so we can find the area of the triangle abc and then double it to find the area of the square.

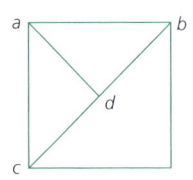

The diagonal $|bc| = 14$, as it is the diameter of the circle.

The length $ad = 7$, as it is a radius.

Area of triangle abc = $\frac{1}{2}$ base by perpendicular height.

$$= \frac{1}{2}(14)(7) = 49$$

Area of square = $2(49) = 98$

Shaded area = $154 - 98 = 56$ m²

Note: There are many other shapes we could be asked to find the area and perimeter of, which are a combination of the above shapes.

Volume and area of a box

Rectangular box has 6 sides (learn formulae):

$$\text{Volume} = l \times b \times h$$

$$\text{Surface area} = 2(lb + lh + bh)$$

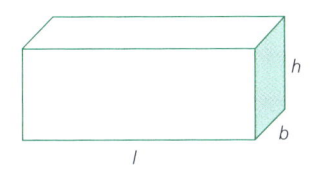

Example: If a rectangular box with an open top has a length of 12 cm, a height of 8 cm and an area of 928 cm², find its breadth.

Solution

Box: $l = 12$, $h = 8$, $A = 928$; find b.

We must be very careful, because as it does not have a top then the formula will have to change.

From the diagram we can see we have two front walls, two sidewalls and only one bottom. The formula has changed.

$$A = lb + 2bh + 2lh$$

put figures in and solve the equation

$$928 = 12b + 2(8b) + 2(12)(8)$$

$$928 = 12b + 20b + 192$$

$$736 = 32b$$

$$32b = 736$$

$$b = 23 \text{ m}$$

Example: The mass of a rectangular sheet of metal is 45,000 grams. The mass of 1 cm³ of this metal is 7.2 grams.

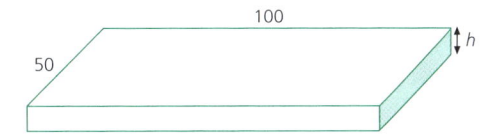

The thickness of the sheet of metal is h cm and its length and width are 100 cm and 50 cm, respectively, as in the diagram. Calculate the value of h.

Solution

We know the total mass and the mass per cm³. We need to turn the grams into cm³ by dividing 45,000 by 7.2.

$$\frac{45000}{7.2} = 6{,}250 \text{ cm}^3$$

Box: $l = 100$, $b = 50$, $V = 6{,}250$; find h.

$$V = l \times b \times h$$

put figures in and work out

$$6{,}250 = (100)(50)h$$

$$5{,}000h = 6{,}250$$

$$h = 1.25 \text{ cm}$$

Cylinders

Two formulae, again in the maths tables, page 7.

$$\text{Curved surface area} = 2\pi r h$$

$$\text{Volume} = \pi r^2 h$$

73

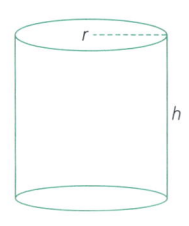

Note: Both of these formulae are in the maths tables, so we do not need to know them but we do have a problem depending on the type of cylinder it is.

> The area of an open cylinder is the same as its surface area.
>
> The area of a closed cylinder is the curved surface area + 2 circles (one on top and the other on the bottom).
>
> The area of an open-top cylinder is the curved area + 1 circle.

Example: A solid cylinder has a radius of 7 cm and height 5 cm. Find its volume and total area when $\pi = \frac{22}{7}$.

Solution

$r = 7, h = 5, \pi = \frac{22}{7}$; find V.

$V = \pi r^2 h$

$V = \frac{22}{7} \left(\frac{7^2}{1}\right)\left(\frac{5}{1}\right)$

use the calculator to find answer

$= 770$ cm^3

Note: This question has 2 parts to it. It is very easy to do one part of a question and forget the second part.

$A = 2\pi r h + 2\pi r^2$

$= \left(\frac{22}{7}\right)\left(\frac{5}{1}\right)\left(\frac{7}{1}\right) + 2\left(\frac{22}{7}\right)\left(\frac{7^2}{1}\right)$

$= 110 + 308 = 418$ cm^2

Example: A solid cylinder has a volume of 4500 π m^3. If the height is 5 m, find the radius.

Solution

$r = ?, h = 5, \pi = \pi, V = 4,500\pi$

$4,500 \pi = \pi r^2 (5)$

cancel π on both sides and swap both sides to have letters on the left

$5r^2 = 4,500$

divide both sides by 5

$r^2 = 900$

to get rid of square, square root both sides

$r = 30$ m

Example: A solid cylinder has an area of 54π m^2 and a radius of 2 m; find its height.

Solution

$A = 54\pi$ m^2 and $r = 2$

$A = 2\pi r h + 2\pi r^2$

put figures instead of letters

$54\pi = 2\pi(2)h + 2\pi(2)^2$

divide every term by π and solve the equation

$54 = 4h + 2(4)$

$54 = 4h + 8$

$46 = 4h$

$4h = 46$

$h = 11.5$ m

Spheres and hemispheres

Two formulae, again in the maths tables on page 7.

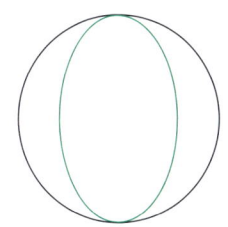

Curved surface area = $4\pi r^2$

Volume = $\frac{4}{3}\pi r^3$

Note: The formulae for a hemisphere are not in the tables.

A hemisphere is half a sphere.

Curved surface area = $2\pi r^2$

Volume = $\frac{2}{3}\pi r^3$

Example: Find the volume of a sphere of radius 4.5 cm in terms of π.

Solution

$r = 4.5$; find V

$V = \frac{4}{3}\pi r^3$

put the figures in

$= \frac{4}{3}\pi(4.5)^3$

cube first (multiply by itself 3 times)

$= \frac{4}{3}\pi(91.125)$

divide by 3 and multiply by 4

$= 121.5\pi$ cm^3

Example: If a solid hemisphere has a volume of 18π m^3, find its radius.

Solution

$V = 18\pi$; find r

$V = \frac{2}{3}\pi r^3$

put figures in

$18\pi = \frac{2}{3}\pi r^3$

divide both sides by π

$\frac{2}{3}r^3 = 18$

multiply across by 3

$2r^3 = 54$

divide by 2

$r^3 = 27$

to get rid of cube, find the cube root

$r = 3$ m

Note: Cube root means we need a number which when multiplied by itself 3 times gives the required answer. Some are easy – cube root of 8 is 2, of 27 is 3 and so on.

Cones

A cone has an extra dimension that we should be aware of, i.e. a slant height of l.

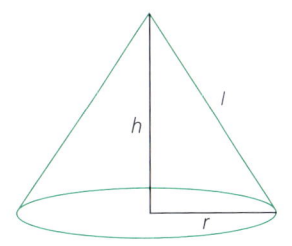

Volume = $\frac{1}{3}\pi r^2 h$

Curved surface area = $\pi r l$

An important property is that $h^2 + r^2 = l^2$.

Example: A solid cone has an area of 24π m^2 and a radius of 3 m. Find its volume in terms of π.

Solution
We are asked to find the volume, but we are given the radius and area. We cannot find the volume without the height. The formula for area will allow us to find the slant height, and then we must use the property above to find the vertical height.

$A = 24\pi$, $r = 3$: find l.

$$A = \pi r l + \pi r^2$$

put figures in

$$24\pi = \pi(3)l + \pi(3)^2$$

divide across by π and solve the equation to find l

$$24 = 3l + 9$$
$$15 = 3l$$
$$l = 5 \text{ m}$$

We new know $r = 3$, $l = 5$: find h.

$$h^2 + r^2 = l^2$$

use Pythagoras' theorem to solve for h.

$$h^2 + 3^2 = 5^2$$
$$h^2 + 9 = 25$$
$$h^2 = 16$$
$$h = 4 \text{ m}$$

$r = 3$, $h = 4$: find V.

$$V = \frac{1}{3}\pi(3)^2 \, 4$$
$$= \frac{1}{3}\pi(9)(4)$$
$$= 12\pi \text{ m}^3$$

Volume of triangular prism, or wedge

Multiplying the front area by the thickness of the object gives the volume.

Example: Find the volume of the triangular wedge as shown.

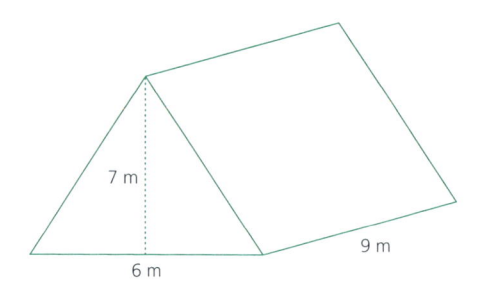

7 m
6 m
9 m

Solution
Area of triangle = half base by perpendicular height.

$$A = \frac{1}{2}(6)(7)$$
$$= 21 \text{ m}^2$$

Volume of wedge = area of front triangle multiplied by thickness

$$V = 21 \times 9$$
$$= 189 \text{ m}^3$$

Recasting

These are questions in which one object is melted down and made into another.

The volume is the same for both objects concerned.

76

Example: A solid cylinder of radius 6 cm and height 9 cm is melted down and recast as a cone of radius 12 cm. Find the height of the cone.

Solution

We need to find the volume of the cylinder in terms of π.

$r = 6$, $h = 9$: find V.

$V = \pi r^2 h$ put figures in

$= \pi(6)^2 9$

square first and then multiply

$= 324\pi$

Cone $r = 6$, $V = 324\pi$: find h.

$V = \frac{1}{3}\pi r^2 h$ put figures in

$324\pi = \frac{1}{3}\pi(12)^2 h$

divide across by π

$324 = \frac{1}{3}(144h)$

$324 = 48h$

$48h = 324$

$h = 6.75$ cm

Moving liquids

When an object is placed in water, the volume of water displaced is equal to the volume of the object.

Example: A cylinder is partially filled with water. The cylinder has a radius of 6 cm. A solid sphere of radius 3 cm is dropped into the cylinder and sinks to the bottom. By how much does the water in the cylinder rise?

Solution

There is some water in the cylinder, but we do not know (or need to know) the height of the water.

The sphere is thrown into the water and the water rises by the same volume as the volume of the sphere.

What we really need is the height of the dark region in the diagram, which is a cylinder of radius 6 cm and has the same volume as the volume of a sphere of radius 3 cm.

Sphere: $r = 3$; find V.

$V = \frac{4}{3}\pi r^3$ put the figures in

$= \frac{4}{3}\pi(3)^3$

cube first (multiply by itself 3 times)

$= \frac{4}{3}\pi(27)$

divide by 3 and multiply by 4

$= 36\pi$

Cylinder: $r = 6$, $V = 36\pi$; find h.

$36\pi = \pi r^2(6)$

cancel π on both sides, swap both sides to have letters on the left

77

$36r^2 = 36$

$r^2 = 1$ divide both sides by 36

to get rid of square, square root both sides

$r = 1$ cm

Flow of liquid

The main formula to remember for these questions is:

$$\text{Time} = \frac{\text{volume}}{\text{rate of flow}}$$

Example: Water flows through a cylindrical pipe of internal diameter 1 cm at a speed of 2 cm per second.

(i) Verify that the rate of flow is $\frac{11}{7}$ cm³ per second, taking $\pi = \frac{22}{7}$.

(ii) The water from the pipe flows into an empty hemispherical bowl. It takes 36 seconds to fill the bowl. Calculate the internal radius of the bowl.

Note: Speed of 2 cm per second means the height of the cylinder is 2 cm.

Solution

(i) To find the rate of flow we need to find the volume of a cylinder, i.e. how much water flows through the pipe per second.

$r = \frac{1}{2}, h = 2, \pi = \frac{22}{7}$; find V.

$V = \pi r^2 h$

$= \frac{22}{7}\left(\frac{1}{2}\right)^2\left(\frac{2}{1}\right)$

$= \frac{22}{7}\left(\frac{1}{4}\right)\left(\frac{2}{1}\right)$

$= \frac{11}{7}$

Volume flowing per second $= \frac{11}{7}$ cm³

(ii) Total water flowing through the cylinder in 36 seconds $= \frac{11}{7} \times 36 = \frac{396}{7}$

Hemisphere: $V = \frac{396}{7}$; find r.

$V = \frac{2}{3}\pi r^3$

$\frac{396}{7} = \frac{2}{3}\left(\frac{22}{7}\right)r^3$ sub figures in

$\frac{396}{7} = \frac{44r^3}{21}$

get the common denominator

$44r^3 = 1188$ letters to the left

$r^3 = 27$

$r = 3$ cm

Shapes within a shape

Example:

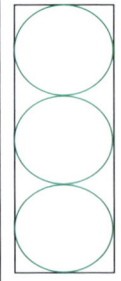

3 spheres of radius 6 cm are placed in the smallest possible cylinder. Find the percentage of empty space in the cylinder.

Solution

Empty space = volume of the cylinder − volume of the three spheres

78

Sphere: $r = 6$

$$V = \frac{4}{3}\pi r^3$$

$$= \frac{4}{3}\pi (6)^3$$

$$= \frac{4}{3}\pi (216)$$

$$= 288\pi$$

Volume of 3 spheres = $3 \times 288\pi = 864\pi$

The main question here is: what is the height of the cylinder? Each of the spheres has a radius of 6 cm and so a diameter of 12 cm. The total height of the cylinder must be 36 cm, since there is one sphere on top of another and each sphere has a radius of 6 and thus a diameter of 12.

Find the volume of the cylinder: $r = 6$, $h = 36$.

$$V = \pi r^2 h$$

$$= \pi(6)^2(36)$$

$$= \pi(36)(36)$$

$$= 1296\pi$$

Empty space = $1296\pi - 864\pi = 432\pi$

Percentage of empty space

$$= \frac{\text{space}}{\text{cylinder}} \times \frac{100}{1} = \frac{432\pi}{1296\pi} \times \frac{100}{1} = 33\%$$

Double shapes

Example: A toy is made of a cone, which fits exactly on top of a hemisphere, as shown in the diagram. The radius length of the hemisphere is 6 cm and the total toy height is 21 cm.

(i) Write down the height of the cone and hence find the volume of the cone in terms of π.

(ii) Find the volume of the hemisphere in terms of π.

(iii) Express the volume of the cone as a percentage of the volume of the total toy, correct to one decimal place.

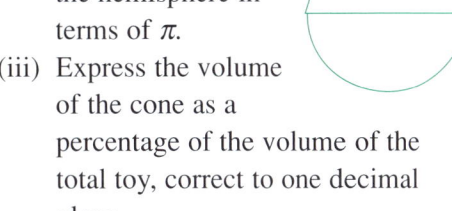

Solution

With double shapes you must:

> State which two shapes you are dealing with.
> Write down what you know about each shape; one length is missing (must be figured out).
> Write down the formula and put figures in.

(i) The total height of the toy is 21 cm and the height of the hemisphere is 6 cm, so the height of the cone must be $21 - 6 = 15$ cm

(ii) Hemisphere: $r = 6$

$$V = \frac{2}{3}\pi r^3$$

$$= \frac{2}{3}\pi (6)^3$$

$$= \frac{2}{3}\pi (216)$$

$$= 144\pi \text{ cm}^3$$

(iii) Cone: $r = 6$ and $h = 15$

$$V = \frac{1}{3}\pi r^2 h$$

$$= \frac{1}{3}\pi r^2 h$$

$$= \pi(36)(15)$$

$$= 540\pi \text{ cm}^3$$

Total $= 144\pi + 540\pi = 684\pi$

Percentage cone $= \dfrac{\text{cone}}{\text{total}} \times \dfrac{100}{1}$

$$= \dfrac{540\pi}{684\pi} \times \dfrac{100}{1}$$

$$= 78.94\%$$

$$= 78.9\%$$

to 1 decimal place

Example: Wax in the shape of a cylinder with radius length 4 cm and height 36 cm is melted down. The resultant wax is formed into cone-shaped candles. Each candle has a height of 6 cm and a base radius length of 2 cm.

(i) Calculate the number of candles that can be made, assuming that no wax is lost.
(ii) The candles are placed, base down and in rows of three, in the smallest possible rectangular box. Calculate, in cm³, the volume of the box.
(iii) What percentage of the volume of the box is empty?

Solution

(i) Cylinder: $r = 4$, $h = 36$; find V.

$$V = \pi r^2 h$$

$$= \pi(4)^2(36)$$

$$= 576\pi$$

Cone: $r = 2, h = 6$; find V.

$$V = \frac{1}{3}\pi r^2 h$$

$$= \frac{1}{3}\pi(2)^2(6)$$

$$= 24\pi$$

Number of candles

$$= \dfrac{\text{volume of cylinder}}{\text{volume of cylinder}} = \dfrac{576}{24\pi} = 24$$

There are 24 candles in rows of three, so there must be 8 rows.

(ii) The box has three dimensions that we must figure out:

The height of the box is the same as the height of the candles = 6 cm.
To figure out the length and breadth, draw the box looking in from the top.

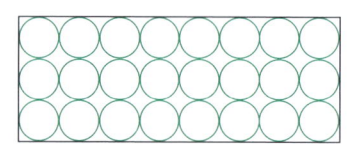

Each sphere has a radius of 2 cm so the thickness (diameter) of each sphere is 4 cm.

The length has 8 spheres side by side so the total length must be $8 \times 4 = 32$ cm.

The width has 3 spheres side by side so the total width must be $3 \times 4 = 12$ cm.

Box: $l = 32$, $b = 12$, $h = 6$; find V.

$$V = l \times b \times h$$

$$= 32 \times 12 \times 6 = 2304 \text{ cm}^3$$

(iii) Empty space = volume of box − volume of 24 candles

$$= 2304 - 24(24\pi)$$

$$= 2304 - 24(24)(3.14)$$

$$= 2304 - 1808.64$$

$$= 495.36 \text{ cm}^3$$

Percentage empty

$$= \frac{\text{empty space}}{\text{volume of the box}} \times \frac{100}{1}$$

$$= \frac{495.36}{2304} \times \frac{100}{1} = 21.5\%$$

Example: A container is in the shape of a cylinder on top of a hemisphere, as shown in the diagram.

The cylinder has a radius of length 3 cm and the container has a total height of 15 cm.

Calculate the volume of the container in terms of π.

If half the volume of the container is filled with liquid, calculate the height, h, of the liquid in the container.

Solution

Cylinder: $r = 3$, $h = 12$; find V.

$$V = \pi r^2 h$$
$$= \pi(3)^2(12)$$
$$= 108\pi$$

Hemisphere: $r = 3$

$$V = \frac{2}{3}\pi r^3$$
$$= \frac{2}{3}\pi(3)^3$$
$$= \frac{2}{3}\pi(27)$$
$$= 18\pi$$

Total volume = $108\pi + 18\pi = 126\pi$ cm^3

Note: The height of the cylinder was not given to us, so we had to figure it out. The total height of the container is 15, but the height of the hemisphere at the bottom is 3. The height of the cylinder must be 15 − 3 = 12 cm.

Half the volume of the container is filled with liquid; volume of water = 63π.

When the water is poured in it is the hemisphere at the bottom that gets filled up first.

The amount of water in the cylindrical part is $63\pi - 18\pi = 45\pi$.

Cylinder: $r = 3$, $V = 45\pi$

$$V = \pi r^2 h$$
$$45\pi = \pi(3)^2(h)$$
$$9h = 45$$
$$h = 5$$

Height of water = 5 + 3 = 8 cm

Example: A grain silo consists of a cylinder and an inverted cone (as in the diagram).

The height of the cylindrical part is 10 m and the radius is 2 m.

The slant height of the cone is 2.5 m.

Find the volume of the silo in terms of π.

When the volume of grain in the silo is 22π m^3, calculate the depth of grain measured from the apex (point) of the cone.

Solution

Cylinder: $r = 2$, $h = 10$; find V.

$$V = \pi r^2 h$$
$$= \pi(2)^2(10)$$
$$= 40\pi$$

Cone: $r = 2$, $l = 2.5$; find h.

$$h^2 + r^2 = l^2$$

use Pythagoras' theorem to solve for h.

$$h^2 + 2^2 = (2.5)^2$$
$$h^2 + 4 = 6.25$$
$$h^2 = 2.25$$
$$h = 1.5 \text{ m}$$

Cone: $r = 2$, $h = 1.5$; find V.

$$V = \tfrac{1}{3}\pi r^2 h$$
$$= \tfrac{1}{3}\pi(2)^2(1.5)$$
$$= 2\pi$$

Volume of container = $40\pi + 2\pi = 42\pi$ m³

Volume of grain in the silo is 22π m³.

The cone at the bottom gets filled up first. The rest of the grain goes into the cylindrical section. There must be $22\pi - 2\pi = 20\pi$ of grain in the cylindrical section.

We have a cylinder with $r = 2$, $V = 20\pi$.

$$V = \pi r^2 h$$
$$20\pi = \pi(2)^2(h)$$
$$4h = 20$$
$$h = 5 \text{ m}$$

Total height of grain is $1.5 + 5 = 6.5$ m

Simpson's Rule

This is used to find the area of odd shapes by using the formula:

Area =
$$\tfrac{\text{gap}}{3} \{\text{first} + \text{last} + 2 \text{ (odd)} + 4(\text{even})\}$$

The best way to remember this is:
TOFE = twice odd + four even.
There are only two types of question that can be asked here.

Type 1

To find the area of an odd shape.

Example:

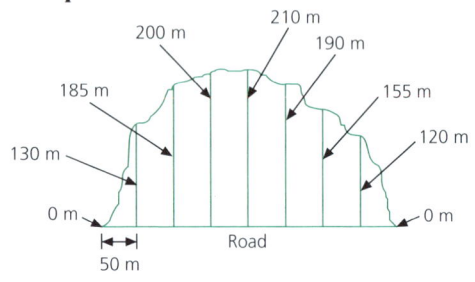

The sketch shows a piece of land covered by forest which lies on one side of a straight road.

At equal intervals of 50 m along the road, perpendicular measurements of 130 m, 185 m, 200 m, 210 m, 190 m, 155 m and 120 m are made to the forest boundary.

Use Simpson's Rule to estimate the area of land covered by the forest.
[See Tables, page 42.]
Give your answer in hectares.
[Note: 1 hectare = 10,000 m².]

Solution

The first thing to do is to mark in on the exam paper each of the heights, as shown.

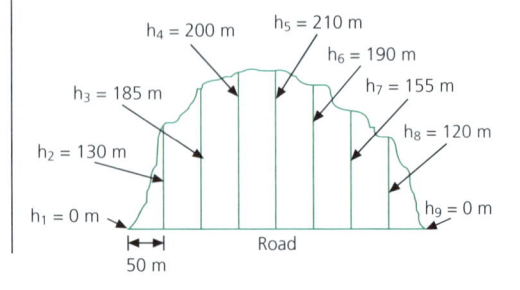

$h_1 = 0$ m
$h_2 = 130$ m
$h_3 = 185$ m
$h_4 = 200$ m
$h_5 = 210$ m
$h_6 = 190$ m
$h_7 = 155$ m
$h_8 = 120$ m
$h_9 = 0$ m

Note: The first height, at the left, is $h_1 = 0$.

Write down the formula:

Area = $\dfrac{\text{gap}}{3}$ {first + last + 2(odd) + 4(even)}

and apply to this question.

The gap between each line is 50

Area = $\dfrac{50}{3}$ {$h_1 + h_9 + 2(h_3 + h_5 + h_7)$
 + $4(h_2 + h_4 + h_6 + h_8)$}

Sub in $h_1 = 0$, $h_2 = 130$, $h_3 = 185$,

$h_4 = 200$, $h_5 = 210$, $h_6 = 190$, $h_7 = 155$,

$h_8 = 120$, $h_9 = 0$

Area = $\dfrac{50}{3}$ {0 + 0 + 2(185 + 210 + 155)
 + 4(130 + 200 + 190 + 120)}

add inside brackets

= $\dfrac{50}{3}$ {(2(550) + 4(640)}

multiply out

= $\dfrac{50}{3}$ {1100 + 2560}

add inside brackets

= $\dfrac{50}{3}$ (3660)

multiply by 50 and then divide by 3

= 61,000

Answer is 61,000 m² but we were told to give the answer in hectares.

We are told that 1 hectare = 10,000 m². To convert 61,000 m² into hectares divide by 10,000 to get 6.1 hectares.

Type 2

Given the area, to find one of the missing lengths.

Example: The diagram shows a sketch of a piece of paper *abcd* with one uneven edge. At equal intervals of h cm along [*bc*], perpendicular measurements of 12 cm, 8 cm, 9 cm, 6 cm, 5 cm, 7 cm and 11 cm are made to the top edge.

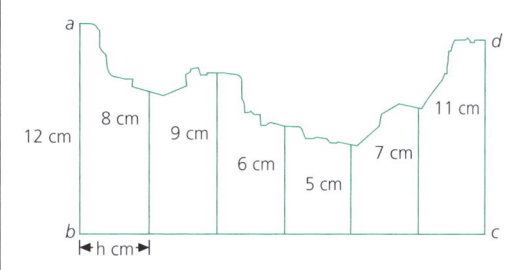

Using Simpson's Rule the area of the piece of paper is estimated to be 180 cm². Calculate the value of h.
[See Tables, page 42.]

Solution

Keep to the same method as above. Mark in on the exam paper each of the heights, as shown.

Write down the formula:

Area

= $\dfrac{\text{gap}}{3}$ {first + last + 2(odd) + 4(even)}

and apply to this question.

83

The gap between each line is unknown and in the question is called h.

Area $= \dfrac{\text{gap}}{3} \{h_1 + h_7 + 2(h_3 + h_5)$
$\qquad\qquad + 4(h_2 + h_4 + h_6)\}$

Sub in $h_1 = 12, h_2 = 8, h_3 = 9, h_4 = 6,$
$h_5 = 5, h_6 = 7, h_7 = 11$

Area $= \dfrac{h}{3} \{12 + 11 + 2(9 + 5)$
$\qquad\qquad + 4(8 + 6 + 7)\}$ add inside brackets

$180 = \dfrac{h}{3}\{23 + 2(14) + 4(21)\}$

multiply out

$180 = \dfrac{h}{3}\{23 + 28 + 84\}$ add

$180 = \dfrac{h}{3}(135)$ divide by 3

$180 = 45h$ letter to left and solve

$45h = 180$

$\quad h = 4$ cm

Chapter 8
The Line

It is always important to remember that when you cannot understand a question, you should try to **draw a diagram** to see what is going on.

You must learn the formulae really well.

Contents

(a) Distance (page 86)
(b) Midpoint (page 87)
(c) Area of a triangle (page 87)
(d) Slope between two points (page 88)
(e) Slope of a given line (page 88)
(f) Parallel and perpendicular lines (page 89)
(g) Equation of a line (page 89)
(h) To find the equation of a line given two points on the line (page 90)
(i) To find the equation of a line parallel or perpendicular to another line (page 91)
(j) To show a point is on a line (page 91)
(k) To draw a line (page 92)
(l) To find where two lines meet (page 92)
(m) To move a point under a given translation (page 93)
(n) To find the image of a line under a given translation (page 93).

Every point has two parts (x, y) called the coordinates.

The x-coordinate always comes first and on a diagram tells us to go left (if negative) or right (if positive).
The y-coordinate comes second and tells us to go down (if negative) or up (if positive).

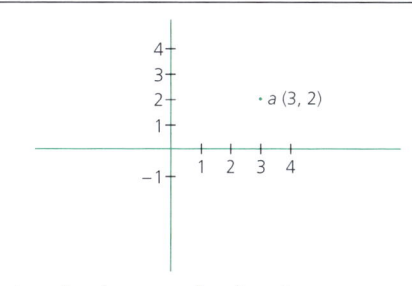

A point is named using lower-case letters and a line is named using capital letters.

When you see $a(3, 2)$ they are talking about the point (3, 2), which is 3 to the right and then up 2.

With each one of the formulae we must follow the steps:

Step 1: Write down the points from the question.

Step 2: Label the points (x_1, y_1) and (x_2, y_2).

Step 3: Write down the formula.

Step 4: Put the figures into the formula and work it out.

Note: As usual, you must take a lot of care with signs.

85

Distance

Distance between two points (x_1, y_1) and (x_2, y_2) is given by:

$$\sqrt{(x_2 - x_1)^2 + (y_2 - y_1)^2}$$

Example: $a(3, -1)$ and $b(-5, 7)$ are two points. Find $|ab|$.

Note: $|ab|$ means the distance from a to b.

Solution

Go through the steps outlined above.
Write down the points and label them

$$(3, -1) \quad (-5, 7)$$
$$(x_1, y_1) \quad (x_2, y_2)$$

write down the formula

$$\sqrt{(x_2 - x_1)^2 + (y_2 - y_1)^2}$$

put figures in and note the double minus

$$\sqrt{(-5-3)^2 + (7-(-1))^2}$$

$$\sqrt{(-8)^2 + (8)^2}$$

square and simplify

$$\sqrt{64 + 64}$$
$$= \sqrt{128}$$

Example: The distance between $(5, 2)$ and $(8, k)$ is 5. Find k.

Solution

Follow the method outlined above at all times.
Write down the points and label them

$$(5, 2) \quad (8, k)$$
$$(x_1, y_1) \quad (x_2, y_2)$$

write down the formula

$$\sqrt{(x_2 - x_1)^2 + (y_2 - y_1)^2}$$

put the figures in and let answer = 5 (from question)

$$\sqrt{(8-5)^2 + (k-2)^2} = 5$$

$$\sqrt{3^2 + (k-2)^2} = 5$$

tidy up and square (note below)

$$\sqrt{9 + k^2 - 4k + 4} = 5$$

add like parts $(9 + 4)$

$$\sqrt{k^2 - 4k + 13} = 5$$

to get rid of $\sqrt{}$ square both sides

$$k^2 - 4k + 13 = 25$$

bring all the terms to the left and solve the quadratic

$$k^2 - 4k - 12 = 0$$
$$(k - 6)(k + 2) = 0$$
$$k - 6 = 0 \quad k + 2 = 0$$
or
$$k = 6 \quad k = -2$$

Note: From algebra we know there is no easy way to do $(k - 2)^2$.

$$(k - 2)^2 = (k - 2)(k - 2)$$
$$= k(k - 2) - 2(k - 2)$$
$$= k^2 - 2k - 2k + 4$$
$$= k^2 - 4k + 4$$

This formula may be needed in a number of different questions, such as:

Show that the triangle $a(2, 3)$, $b(3, -5)$ and $c(-5, -6)$ is isosceles.

Isosceles triangle means that two of the lengths are the same. This means find the distance between a and b, then a and c, then b and c. When you have done this 2 of your distances should be the same.

If it were an equilateral triangle, all 3 distances would be the same.

Midpoint

The midpoint between two given points is given by:
$$\left(\frac{x_1 + x_2}{2}, \frac{y_1 + y_2}{2}\right)$$

Example: Find the midpoint of (–3, 4) and (9, –8).

Solution

(–3, 4) and (9, –8)
(x_1, y_1) (x_2, y_2)

Write down the formula

$$\left(\frac{x_1 + x_2}{2}, \frac{y_1 + y_2}{2}\right)$$

$\left(\frac{-3 + 9}{2}, \frac{4 + (-8)}{2}\right)$ put figures in

work out the two separate points

$$\left(\frac{6}{2}, \frac{-4}{2}\right)$$

$= (3, -2)$

Example: If m(3, 7) is the midpoint of [pq] where p is (6, 5), find q.

Solution

This time we are given the midpoint to find one of the missing end points.

Method 1: Let q be (x, y) and continue as normal.

(3, 7) and (x, y)
(x_1, y_1) (x_2, y_2)

write down the formula

$$\left(\frac{x_1 + x_2}{2}, \frac{y_1 + y_2}{2}\right)$$

put figures in and let answers = (3, 7)

$$\left(\frac{6 + x}{2}, \frac{5 + y}{2}\right) = (3, 7)$$

$\frac{6 + x}{2} = 3$ $\frac{5 + y}{2} = 7$

$6 + x = 6$ $5 + y = 14$

$x = 0$ $y = 9$

Method 2: If we read the question carefully we see that m(3, 7) is in the centre of p(6, 5) and q, so that we can do a central symmetry from p through m and on to find q.

x-coordinates   6 $\xrightarrow{\text{down 3 to}}$ 3 $\xrightarrow{\text{down 3 to}}$ 0

y-coordinates   5 $\xrightarrow{\text{up 2 to}}$ 7 $\xrightarrow{\text{up 2 to}}$ 9

Answer therefore is (0, 9)

Area of a triangle

The area of a triangle where one of the vertices must be (0, 0) is:
$$\text{Area} = \frac{1}{2}|x_1 y_2 - x_2 y_1|$$

Note: The two lines on either side mean that the answer must be positive.

Note: Vertices are the corner points of a triangle.

Example: Find the area of (–2, 4), (1, –3) and (6, –2)

Solution

We must move one of the points onto (0, 0) by using what is called a translation. This means we look at the x- and then the y-coordinates and see by how much they

87

have changed. We make this into a rule, which we then apply to the other points.

The x values go from -2 to 0, so they have gone up by 2.

The y values have gone from 4 to 0, so they have gone down by 4.

$(-2, 4) \rightarrow (0, 0)$ x up by 2, y down by 4

$(1, -3) \rightarrow (3, -7)$ x up by 2, y down by 4

$(6, -2) \rightarrow (8, -6)$ x up by 2, y down by 4

$$(3, -7) \text{ and } (8, -6)$$
$$(x_1, y_1) \quad (x_2, y_2)$$

$$\text{Area} = \tfrac{1}{2}|x_1 y_2 - x_2 y_1|$$

put the figures in; $x_1 y_2$ means multiply 3 by -6

$$= \tfrac{1}{2}|3(-6) - 8(-7)|$$

multiply first and then add or subtract

$$= \tfrac{1}{2}|-18 + 56|$$

$$= \tfrac{1}{2}|38| = 19 \text{ sq units}$$

Slope between two points

Slope of a line between two given points is given by:
$$m = \frac{y_2 - y_1}{x_2 - x_1}$$

Example: Find slope between $a(2, -3)$ and $b(3, -1)$.

Solution

$$a(2, -3) \text{ and } b(3, -1)$$
$$(x_1, y_1) \quad (x_2, y_2)$$

$$m = \frac{y_2 - y_1}{x_2 - x_1} \quad \text{write down formula}$$

put figures in and take care over the signs

$$= \frac{-1 - (-3)}{3 - 2}$$

$$= \frac{-1 + 3}{1} = 2$$

Note: Always leave slope as a whole number or a fraction.

Slope of a given line

Slope of the line
$ax + by + c = 0$ is $m = -\dfrac{a}{b}$

Note: To find the slope of a line, it comes down to:

$$\text{minus } \frac{\text{number in front of } x}{\text{number in front of } y}$$

Note: The textbooks use the idea that we write the line in the form $y = mx + c$ and the slope will be the number in front of the x.

Example: Find the slope of $2x + 3y = 7$.

Solution
$$m = -\tfrac{2}{3}$$

Example: Find the slope of $x - 3y = 9$.

Solution
$$m = -\frac{1}{-3}$$

two minus signs make a plus

$$= \tfrac{1}{3}$$

Note: If there is no number in front of the x, then the number in front is 1.

Example: Write $2x + 3y = 7$ in the form $y = mx + c$ and hence find the slope.

Solution

This is a manipulation as done in the algebra notes, where we want to leave y on its own on the left-hand side.

$2x + 3y = 7$ bring the $2x$ to right

$\quad 3y = 7 - 2x$ if a term crosses the equals it changes sign

$\quad y = \frac{7}{3} - \frac{2}{3}x$ to get rid of multiplication divide across by 3

Slope is the number in front of the x, so $m = -\frac{2}{3}$.

Parallel and perpendicular lines

If two lines are parallel, $M \| L$, then the slopes are equal, so $m_1 = m_2$.

If two lines are perpendicular, $L \perp M$, then $m_1 m_2 = -1$.

Note: If we are given a slope and asked to find a parallel slope, then the answer is the exact same as for the first slope.

Note: If we are given a slope and asked to find a perpendicular slope, then the answer is got by inverting and changing sign of the original slope.

Example: If the line L has the following slope, find the slope of the lines parallel and perpendicular to L.

Solution

If L has slope $m = \frac{2}{3}$ then the parallel slope is $m = \frac{2}{3}$, but the perpendicular slope is $m = -\frac{3}{2}$.

If M has slope $m = -\frac{5}{4}$ then the parallel slope is $m = -\frac{5}{4}$, but the perpendicular slope is $m = \frac{4}{5}$.

If N has slope $m = 6$ then the parallel slope is $m = 6$, but the perpendicular slope is $m = -\frac{1}{6}$.

Example: L is the line $3x - 7y = 13$ and M is the line $7x + 3y = 21$. Prove that $L \perp M$.

Solution

$$\text{Slope of } L \text{ is } m_1 = -\frac{3}{-7} = \frac{3}{7}$$

$$\text{Slope of } M \text{ is } m_2 = -\frac{7}{3}$$

$L \perp M$ since $m_1 m_2 = \left(\frac{3}{7}\right)\left(-\frac{7}{3}\right) = -1$

Equation of a line

The equation of a line is given by:
$$y - y_1 = m(x - x_1)$$

Note: To be able to use this formula we must be given two pieces of information:

(a) one point on the line
(b) slope of the line.

Example: Find the equation of a line containing the point (2, –5) and with slope $m = -\frac{3}{7}$.

Solution

Use the point (2, –5) and $m = -\frac{3}{7}$ in the formula $y - y_1 = m(x - x_1)$

put figures in, be careful of double minus

$$y - (-5) = -\frac{3}{7}(x - 2)$$

cross-multiply by 7

$$7(y + 5) = -3(x - 2)$$

multiply out brackets

$$7y + 35 = -3x + 6$$

letters to left, numbers to right

$$3x + 7y = -29$$

To find the equation of a line given two points on the line

Step 1: Find slope between the two given points.

Step 2: Using one point and slope, find equation of line.

Example: $a(1, 3)$ and $b(4, -5)$ are two points. Find the equation of the line ab.

Solution

Must find the slope between

$a(1, 3)$ and $b(4, -5)$

(x_1, y_1) (x_2, y_2)

$m = \frac{y_2 - y_1}{x_2 - x_1}$ write down formula

$= \frac{-5 - 3}{4 - 1}$ put figures in and take care of the signs

$= \frac{-8}{3} = -\frac{8}{3}$

Use the point $a(1, 3)$ and $m = -\frac{8}{3}$ in the formula $y - y_1 = m(x - x_1)$

$y - 3 = -\frac{8}{3}(x - 1)$ put figures in

$3(y - 3) = -8(x - 1)$ cross-multiply by 3

$3y - 9 = -8x + 8$ multiply out brackets

$8x + 3y = 17$ letters to left, numbers to right

Note: It does not matter which point we use, so we could have done the same with the point $b(4, -5)$ and got the right answer.

Example: $a(5, 6)$, $b(-3, -4)$ and $c(-1, 1)$ are three points.

(i) The line L is parallel to bc and passes through a. Find the equation of L.
(ii) The line M is perpendicular to bc and passes through a. Find the equation of M.

Solution

(i) Must find the slope between
$b(-3, -4)$ and $c(-1, 1)$
(x_1, y_1) (x_2, y_2)

$m = \frac{y_2 - y_1}{x_2 - x_1}$ write down formula

$= \frac{1 - (-4)}{-1 - (-3)}$ put figures in and take care of the signs

$= \frac{1 + 4}{-1 + 3} = \frac{5}{2}$

Note: Parallel means use the same slope.

(ii) Use the point $a(5, 6)$ and $m = \dfrac{5}{2}$ in the formula $y - y_1 = m(x - x_1)$

$y - 6 = \dfrac{5}{2}(x - 5)$ put figures in

$2(y - 6) = 5(x - 5)$ cross-multiply by 2

$2y - 12 = 5x - 25$ multiply out brackets

$-5x + 2y = -13$ letters to left, numbers to right

$5x - 2y = 13$ change the sign of the line

Note: Perpendicular means turn upside down (invert) and change sign.

Use the point $a(5, 6)$ and $m = -\dfrac{2}{5}$ in the formula $y - y_1 = m(x - x_1)$

$y - 6 = -\dfrac{2}{5}(x - 5)$

$5(y - 6) = -2(x - 5)$

$5y - 30 = -2x + 10$

$2x + 5y = 40$

To find the equation of a line parallel or perpendicular to another line

Step 1: Find the slope of the given line.
Step 2: Find the slope of the required line.
Step 3: Use the equation-of-line formula.

Example: L is the line $3x + 4y = 16$. M is the line through $(-2, 5)$ which is perpendicular to L. Find the equation of M.

Solution

Find the slope of $L : 3x + 4y = 16$

Slope = minus $\dfrac{\text{number in front of } x}{\text{number in front of } y}$

$\Rightarrow m = -\dfrac{3}{4}$

Since $L \perp M$, then slope of M is $m = \dfrac{4}{3}$

Use the point $(-2, 5)$ and $m = \dfrac{4}{3}$ in the formula $y - y_1 = m(x - x_1)$

$y - 5 = \dfrac{4}{3}(x - (-2))$

$3(y - 5) = 4(x + 2)$

$3y - 15 = 4x + 8$

$-4x + 3y = 23$

$4x - 3y = -23$

To show a point is on a line

Put the given values of x and y into the line and it should satisfy the line, i.e. should work out.

Example: If $(3, 2)$ is on $5x - 6y = k$, find the value of k.

Solution

This is very simple if we follow the method outline, so sub in $x = 3$ and $y = 2$.

$5(3) - 6(2) = k$

$15 - 12 = k$

$3 = k$

To draw a line

Find where it cuts (intercepts) the *x*-axis
On x-axis, y = 0

Find where it cuts (intercepts) the *y*-axis
On y-axis, x = 0

The method here comes down to two parts.

> To find where a line cuts the *x*-axis, put $y = 0$ into the equation and get a value for *x*.
>
> To find where a line cuts the *y*-axis, put $x = 0$ into the equation and get a value for *y*.

Note: Remember we need only 2 points to draw a line.

Example: Draw the line $x + 2y = 4$.

Solution

Find where it cuts the *x*-axis, so sub in $y = 0$ to get $x = 4$. One point is $(4, 0)$.

Find where it cuts the *y*-axis, so sub in $x = 0$ to get $2y = 4$ so $y = 2$. One point is $(0, 2)$.

Draw line.

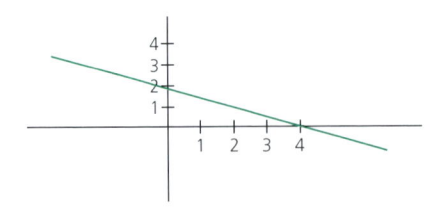

Example: Draw the line $x + 2y = 0$.

Solution

Find where it cuts the *x*-axis, so sub in $y = 0$ to get $x = 0$. One point is $(0, 0)$.
It is of no use to put in $x = 0$ because we get the same point, so put in any other value of *x*.

Sub in $x = 2$ to get $2 + 2y = 0 \Rightarrow y = -1$. Second point is $(2, -1)$.

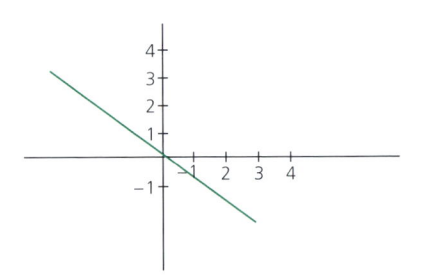

Special lines

> Lines that are horizontal have equation $y =$ a number.
>
> Lines that are vertical have equation $x =$ a number.

Example: Draw the lines $x = 3$ and $y = -2$.

Solution

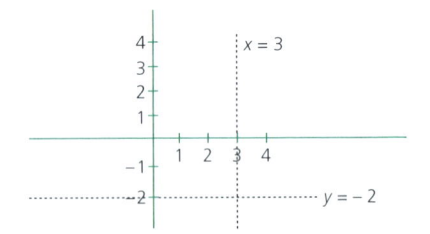

To find where two lines meet

> Use simultaneous equations as from algebra.

92

Example: L is the line $2x + 3y = 8$ and M is the line $x - 2y = -3$. Find p where L and M intersect.

Solution

$$2x + 3y = 8$$
$$x - 2y = -3$$

Multiply the top line by 2 and the bottom by 3 to get

$$4x + 6y = 16$$
$$\underline{3x - 6y = -9}$$ the signs in front of the ys are different, so add all the terms
$$7x \quad = 7$$ divide across by the number in front of the x to get
$$x \quad = 1$$

Put $x = 1$ back into the top equation

$$2(1) + 3y = 8$$
$$2 + 3y = 8$$
$$3y = 6$$
$$y = 2$$

The answer is $p(1, 2)$.

To move a point under a given translation

> Always attempt to make a rule out of the given translation.

We have already used this to find the area of a triangle, but it can be used to find the fourth point in a parallelogram.

Example: $a(-1, 1)$, $b(1, 2)$, $c(2, -1)$, and $d(x, y)$ are four vertices in a parallelogram $abcd$. Find d.

Solution

Always make a rough diagram of the given question.

From the diagram we can see that d is in the left-hand corner and that the movement from b to a is the same as going from c to d.

$(1, 2) \rightarrow (-1, 1)$

x down by 2, y down by 1

$(2, -1) \rightarrow (0, -2)$

x down by 2, y down by 1

Answer is $d(0, -2)$

Note: If you are asked to find the area of a parallelogram, find the area of a triangle and double.

To find the image of a line under a given translation

The slope of a line does not change under a translation. The result is a parallel line.

Step 1: Find the slope of the given line.

Step 2: Find a point on the given line.

Step 3: Find the image of the point from step 2 under the given translation.

Step 4: Using the slope found and the point found, use the equation of a line to find the answer.

Example: *L* is the line $2x - y = -5$. Find the equation of the line *M*, which is the image of *L* under the translation $a(5, -3)$ onto $b(4, -1)$.

Solution

Find the slope of *L*: $2x - y = -5$

$$\text{Slope} = \text{minus } \frac{\text{number in front of } x}{\text{number in front of } y}$$

$$\Rightarrow m = -\frac{2}{-1} = 2$$

Slope of *M* is $m = 2$.

Find a point on $2x - y = -5$.

Let $x = 0$. We get $y = 5$, so one point is $(0, 5)$

$(5, -3) \rightarrow (4, -1)$ *x* down by 1, *y* up by 2

$(0, 5) \rightarrow (-1, 7)$ *x* down by 1, *y* up by 2

Use the point $(-1, 7)$ and $m = 2$ in the formula $y - y_1 = m(x - x_1)$

$$y - 7 = 2(x - (-1))$$
$$y - 7 = 2x + 2$$
$$-2x + y = 9$$
$$2x - y = -9$$

Central symmetry

Definition – move through a point and go the same distance again the other side.

Example: Find image of $(5, -2)$ under central symmetry in $(3, -1)$

Solution

x-coordinates

$5 \xrightarrow{\text{down 2 to}} 3 \xrightarrow{\text{down 2 to}} 1$

y-coordinates

$-2 \xrightarrow{\text{up 1 to}} -1 \xrightarrow{\text{up 1 to}} 0$

Answer therefore is $(1, 0)$.

Axial symmetry

Definition – move through a line at right angles and go the same distance again the other side.

Axial symmetry in the *x*-axis
= change the sign of *y*.
Axial symmetry in the *y*-axis
= change the sign of *x*.
Central symmetry in the origin
= change the sign of *x* and *y*.

The 3 rules above hold whether we are talking about a line or just a point.

Example: Find the image of $(3, 1)$ under (i) S_x (ii) S_y (iii) S_o.

Solution

(i) S_x axial symmetry in the *x*-axis
= change sign of *y*. Ans: $(3, -1)$

(ii) S_y axial symmetry in the *y*-axis
= change sign of *x*. Ans: $(-3, 1)$

(iii) S_o central symmetry in the origin
= change sign of *x* and *y*. Ans: $(-3, -1)$

Chapter 9
The Circle

Contents

(a) Equation of a circle centre (0, 0), radius *r* (page 95)
(b) To find whether a point is inside, on or outside a circle (page 96)
(c) Intersection of a line and a circle (page 97)
(d) To show a line is a tangent to a circle (page 98)
(e) To find a tangent to a circle (page 98)
(f) To find where a circle cuts the axes (page 99)
(g) General equation of a circle centre (*h*, *k*) and radius *r* (page 100)
(h) To find the image of a circle under a transformation (page 103).

This is question 3 on Paper 2. It can be a hard enough question, with some of the (c) parts particularly difficult, but there are only 2 formulae that you need to know in order to get the (a) and (b) parts right. You must know the line notes before you look at this section, as a lot of the ideas are repeated here.

Notation

Centre – this is the exact *midpoint* of the circle.
Radius – this is the *distance* from the centre to any point on the circle.
Diameter – this is a line through the centre from one side of the circle to the other.
Chord – this is a *line* that hits the circle at *two points* but does not necessarily go through the centre. The diameter is a special chord.
Tangent – this is a *line* that hits the outside of the circle at *one point only*.

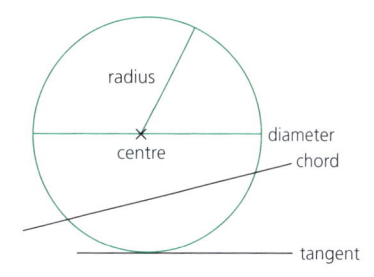

The two most important parts of the circle to be able to find are the centre and radius.

Equation of a circle, centre (0, 0), radius *r*

This is given by the formula:

$$x^2 + y^2 = r^2$$

95

Example: Find the equation of the circle with centre (0, 0) which contains the point (2, –3).

Solution

A quick way is to say that if (2, –3) is on $x^2 + y^2 = r^2$ then you can sub in $x = 2$ and $y = -3$ to find r.

$$x^2 + y^2 = r^2$$

just like the line, sub the point in

$$2^2 + (-3)^2 = r^2$$

square first, then add

$$13 = r^2$$

$$r = \sqrt{13}$$

Circle is $x^2 + y^2 = 13$

Note: You must put the –3 in brackets and remember that when you square a negative it becomes a positive.

Example: Write down the centre and radius of $x^2 + y^2 = 25$.

Solution

Typical (a) part. Since the circle is written in the form $x^2 + y^2 = r^2$ (it looks nearly the same except the question has 25 instead of r^2), you can take one look at this and say centre (0, 0), radius of 5.

Note: Once you see an equation like this, write down centre and radius even if not asked to directly, and you will get at least attempt marks.

To find whether a point is inside, on, or outside a circle

Is the point (x_1, y_1) in, on or outside $x^2 + y^2 = r^2$? Three possible outcomes, but the method is to **substitute** the coordinates of the point into the circle.

> If $(x_1)^2 + (y_1)^2 < r^2$ then the point is inside the circle.
> If $(x_1)^2 + (y_1)^2 = r^2$ then the point is on the circle.
> If $(x_1)^2 + (y_1)^2 > r^2$ then the point is outside the circle.

Example: Determine whether (4, 6) and (–8, 7) are inside, on, or outside the circle $x^2 + y^2 = 100$.

Solution

This is a circle with centre (0, 0) and radius of 10.

Substitute (4, 6), so $x = 4$ and $y = 6$.

$16 + 36 = 52 < 100$

so (4, 6) is inside the circle

$(-8)^2 + (7)^2$

$64 + 49 = 113 > 100$

so (–8, 7) is outside the circle

Example: Name 3 points on the circle $x^2 + y^2 = 49$.

Solution

This is a circle with centre (0, 0) and radius of 7.

Since the radius is 7, we can use this in 3 combinations to find 3 points.

(7, 0), (0, 7), and (–7, 0)

They could have asked us to find 3 points inside the circle $x^2 + y^2 = 49$, so we use small numbers that when we square and add will add to less than 49:

(0, 0) (1, 0) and (0, 1) There are a lot more answers, but these are easy ones.

Example: If the point $(t, 2t)$ is on the circle $x^2 + y^2 = 20$, find two values of t.

Solution

Since the point is on the circle, then substitute it in.

Substitute $x = t$ and $y = 2t$ to form an equation. Put the $2t$ in brackets before squaring

$$t^2 + (2t)^2 = 20$$
$$t^2 + 4t^2 = 20$$

add like terms

$$5t^2 = 20 \quad \text{divide by 5}$$
$$t^2 = 4$$

to get rid of a square, must square root.

$$t = \pm 2$$

Intersection of a line and a circle

Step 1: Get x on its own with the line (or y on its own).
Step 2: Substitute this value for x into the equation of the circle and solve.
Step 3: Put the resultant values for y back into the line to get the values for x.

Example: Find the points of intersection of the line $x + 2y = 5$ and the circle $x^2 + y^2 = 10$.

Solution

Circle $x^2 + y^2 = 10$ has centre (0, 0) and radius $\sqrt{10}$

Step 1: Start with the equation that has no squares and write as either

$$x = \text{ or } y =$$
$$x + 2y = 5$$

leave the x on its own on the left-hand side

$$x = 5 - 2y$$

when a term crosses the equals it changes sign

Step 2: Sub $x = 5 - 2y$ into the circle $x^2 + y^2 = 10$

$$x^2 + y^2 = 10$$

replace the x and put in $5 - 2y$

$$(5 - 2y)^2 + y^2 = 10$$

square means multiplied by itself

$$(5 - 2y)(5 - 2y) + y^2 = 10$$

split the brackets and do not lose the y^2

$$5(5 - 2y) - 2y(5 - 2y) + y^2 = 10$$

multiply out

$$25 - 10y - 10y + 4y^2 + y^2 = 10$$

bring everything to left-hand side

$$25 - 20y + 5y^2 - 10 = 0$$

this has turned into a quadratic

$$5y^2 - 20y + 15 = 0$$

divide across by 5 to make life easier

$$y^2 - 4y + 3 = 0$$

nice easy quadratic; look back to algebra to see 2 different ways to finish

$$y^2 - 1y - 3y - 3 = 0$$

guide number of 3 and add to 4

$$y(y - 1) - 3(y - 1) = 0$$

take out what's common

$$(y - 1)(y - 3) = 0$$

let each bracket = 0

$$y - 1 = 0 \text{ or } y - 3 = 0$$
$$y = 1 \text{ or } y = 3$$

Step 3:

Sub $y = 1$ into the line $x = 5 - 2y$

$$x = 5 - 2(1)$$
$$x = 5 - 2 = 3 \qquad \text{One point is } (3, 1)$$

Sub $y = 3$ into the line $x = 5 - 2y$

$$x = 5 - 2(3)$$
$$x = 5 - 6 = -1 \qquad \text{Other point is } (-1, 3)$$

Points of intersection are $(3, 1)$ and $(-1, 3)$.

To show a line is a tangent to a circle

If a line is a tangent to a circle, then there is only one point of contact. We do the exact same method as above, but we should come up with only one answer.

Example: Is the line $x - 2y = 5$ a tangent to the circle $x^2 + y^2 = 5$?

Solution: The intersection of the line and circle should be a single point. Circle centre $(0, 0)$, radius $\sqrt{5}$

Step 1: $x = 2y + 5$ from the line.

Step 2: Sub this value for x into the circle to find the point(s) of contact.

$$(2y + 5)^2 + y^2 = 5$$
$$(2y + 5)(2y + 5) + y^2 = 5$$
$$2y(2y + 5) + 5(2y + 5) + y^2 = 5$$
$$4y^2 + 10y + 10y + 25 + y^2 = 5$$
$$4y^2 + 20y + 25 + y^2 = 5$$
$$5y^2 + 20y + 25 - 5 = 0$$
$$5y^2 + 20y + 20 = 0$$
$$y^2 + 4y + 4 = 0$$
$$(y + 2)(y + 2) = 0$$
$$y + 2 = 0$$
$$y = -2$$

Step 3: Sub $y = -2$ into the line $x - 2y = 5$

$$x + 4 = 5$$
$$x = 1$$

There is only one point of contact, namely $(1, -2)$, so the line is a tangent to the circle.

To find a tangent to a circle at a given point of contact

Step 1: Find the centre of the circle.
Step 2: Find the slope between centre and given point of contact.
Step 3: Invert and change sign of the slope; we have to find the slope of the tangent.
Step 4: Use given point and slope of tangent in the equation of line to find the tangent.

Example: Find the tangent to $x^2 + y^2 = 25$ at the point $(-3, 4)$ and find the parallel tangent.

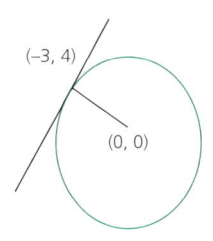

Solution

Step 1: Centre of circle is $(0, 0)$; the radius is $\sqrt{25} = 5$

Step 2: Slope between $(0, 0)$ and $(-3, 4)$

$$\underset{(x_1, y_1)}{} \quad \underset{(x_2, y_2)}{}$$

$$\text{Slope} = \frac{y_2 - y_1}{x_2 - x_1} = \frac{4 - 0}{-3 - 0} = \frac{4}{-3} = -\frac{4}{3}$$

always put the minus on top

Step 3: Slope of tangent $m = \frac{3}{4}$ (invert and change the sign of last slope which was $-\frac{4}{3}$)

Step 4: Use the point $(-3, 4)$ and $m = \frac{3}{4}$ in the formula $y - y_1 = m(x - x_1)$.

Put figures in, be careful of double minus

$$y - 4 = \frac{3}{4}(x - (-3))$$

cross-multiply by 4

$$4(y - 4) = 3(x + 3)$$

multiply out brackets

$$4y - 16 = 3x + 9$$

letters to left, numbers to right

$$-3x + 4y = 25$$

change sign of line to leave x first and positive

$$3x - 4y = -25$$

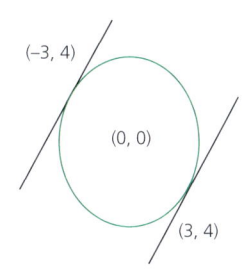

The other tangent we require is parallel, so it has the same slope. We need to find a point on the line. If you look at the rough diagram you can see that $(0, 0)$ is the centre of the circle, so if we move $(-3, 4)$ through $(0, 0)$ and do the same again the other side, we end up at the point $(3, -4)$ which must be on the line we require.

Use the point $(3, -4)$ and $m = \frac{3}{4}$ in the formula:

$$y - (-4) = \frac{3}{4}(x - 3)$$

$$4(y + 4) = 3(x - 3)$$

$$4y + 16 = 3x - 9$$

$$-3x + 4y = -25$$

$$3x - 4y = 25$$

To find where a circle cuts the axes

Example: Find coordinates of the points where $x^2 + y^2 = 81$ cuts the x-axis and find the tangents at these points.

Solution

Centre $(0, 0)$ and radius of $r = 9$

Remember, for a line or circle that cuts

the x-axis $y = 0$

y-axis $x = 0$

$$x^2 = 81$$

to get rid of the square, square root both sides

$$x = \pm 9$$

(remember the square root can be positive or negative).

Circle cuts the x-axis at the points $(9, 0)$ and $(-9, 0)$.

The best way to find the tangents is to draw a diagram:

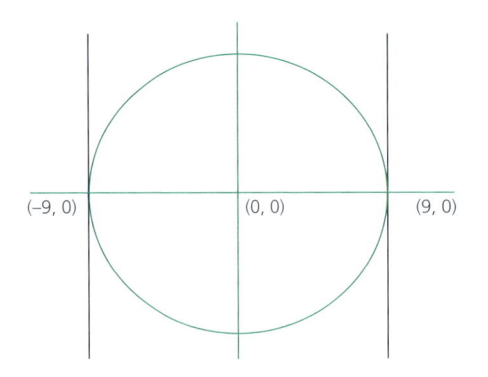

[Diagram showing a circle centred at (0, 0) with points (-9, 0), (0, 0) and (9, 0) marked]

Note 1: Tangents must be vertical lines.
Note 2: Any vertical line is written as $x = a$ number.

The required answers to this question are $x = -9$ and $x = 9$.

Up to now we have dealt only with the equation of a circle which has a centre of $(0, 0)$, but this is not true for all circles; so now we move onto the second type of circle, which has a centre of (h, k). The main thing to remember here is that the methods we have used so far are exactly the same, but the centre is no longer $(0, 0)$.

General equation of a circle, centre (*h*, *k*) and radius *r*

Equation of a circle centre (h, k), radius r, is given by:

$$(x - h)^2 + (y - k)^2 = r^2$$

Example: Find the centre and radius of $(x - 3)^2 + (y + 5)^2 = 17$.

Show that the point $(2, -1)$ is on this circle and find the tangent at this point.

Solution

This is of the form $(x - h)^2 + (y - k)^2 = r^2$, which has centre (h, k) and radius r.

Write the question $(x - 3)^2 + (y + 5)^2 = 17$ under the formula (always write the formula down).

It should be easy to see that the centre is $(3, -5)$ (change the sign of the number after the x and the number after the y)

$$r^2 = 17$$
$$r = \sqrt{17}$$

To show $(2, -1)$ is on the circle, sub $x = 2$ and $y = -1$ into $(x - 3)^2 + (y + 5)^2 = 17$.

$$(2 - 3)^2 + (-1 + 5)^2$$
$$(-1)^2 + 4^2 = 1 + 16 = 17$$

$\Rightarrow (2, -1)$

is on the circle.

To find the tangent, follow the method outlined above.

Example: (i) Find the slope between
(2, −1) and (3, −5)
(x_1, y_1) (x_2, y_2)

Solution

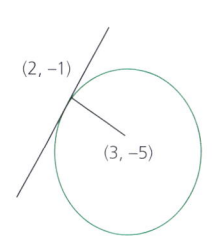

$$m = \frac{y_2 - y_1}{x_2 - x_1} = \frac{-5 - (-1)}{3 - 2}$$

$$= \frac{-5 + 1}{1} = -\frac{4}{1}$$

Slope of tangent is therefore $= \frac{1}{4}$.

(ii) Find the equation of the tangent with slope $m = \frac{1}{4}$ and point $(x_1, y_1) = (2, -1)$.

Solution

$$y - y_1 = m(x - x_1)$$

$$y - (-1) = \frac{1}{4}(x - 2)$$

$$4(y + 1) = x - 2$$

$$4y + 4 = x - 2$$

$$-x + 4y = -6$$

$$x - 4y = 6$$

Example: Find the equation of a circle which has the line segment from (−2, 5) to (4, −1) as a diameter.

Solution

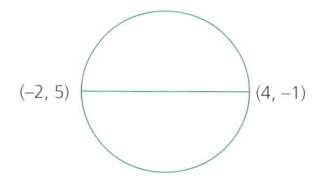

Must find (a) centre (b) radius, and then (c) use the general equation formula.

(a) Centre = midpoint between the points
(− 2, 5) and (4, −1)
(x_1, y_1) (x_2, y_2)

$$\left(\frac{x_1 + x_2}{2}, \frac{y_1 + y_2}{2}\right) = \left(\frac{-2 + 4}{2}, \frac{5 + (-1)}{2}\right)$$

$$= \left(\frac{2}{2}, \frac{4}{2}\right) = (1, 2)$$

(b) Radius = distance from centre (1, 2) to point (−2, 5) (or point (4, −1))

$$\sqrt{(x_2 - x_1)^2 + (y_2 - y_1)^2}$$

$$= \sqrt{(-2 - 1)^2 + (5 - 2)^2}$$

$$= \sqrt{(-3)^2 + 3^2} = \sqrt{9 + 9} = \sqrt{18}$$

(c) Use general equation:

$(x - h)^2 + (y - k)^2 = r^2$
centre $(h, k) = (1, 2)$ and radius $r = \sqrt{18}$

$$(x - 1)^2 + (y - 2)^2 = 18$$

Note: $(\sqrt{18})^2 = 18$ (the square and the square root cancel each other out).

Example: The equation of the circle K is $(x - 3)^2 + (y + 2)^2 = 29$. Find the coordinates of the two points where K intersects the x-axis.

Solution

Cuts the x-axis, so sub in $y = 0$

$$(x - 3)^2 + (0 + 2)^2 = 29$$

$$(x - 3)^2 + 2^2 = 29$$

square means multiply by itself

101

$(x - 3)(x - 3) + 4 = 29$

split the brackets

$x(x - 3) - 3(x - 3) + 4 = 29$

multiply out and bring everything to left

$x^2 - 3x - 3x + 9 + 4 - 29 = 0$

tidy up

$x^2 - 6x - 16 = 0$

quadratic to solve. Guide number –16, subtract to –6

$x^2 - 8x + 2x - 16 = 0$

$x(x - 8) + 2(x - 8) = 0$

$(x + 2)(x - 8) = 0$

$x + 2 = 0 \qquad x - 8 = 0$

or

$x = -2 \qquad x = 8$

Example: $a(7, 3)$, $b(5, -1)$ and $c(9, -3)$ are three points.

(i) Show that the triangle abc is right-angled.
(ii) Hence, find the centre of the circle that passes through a, b and c and write down the equation of the circle.

Solution

The best way to prove that the triangle is a right-angled one is to find the slope between ab and bc. Then use the formula that if two lines are perpendicular, then $m_1 \times m_2 = -1$, where m_1 is the slope of one line (ab) and m_2 is the slope of the second line (bc).

(i) Slope between $a(7, 3)$ and $b(5, -1)$
    $\quad\quad (x_1, y_1) \quad\quad (x_2, y_2)$

$m_1 = \dfrac{y_2 - y_1}{x_2 - x_1} = \dfrac{-1 - 3}{5 - 7} = \dfrac{-4}{-2} = 2$

Leave answer as a whole number when possible.

Slope between $b(5, -1)$ and $c(9, -3)$
    $\quad\quad (x_1, y_1) \quad\quad (x_2, y_2)$

$m_2 = \dfrac{y_2 - y_1}{x_2 - x_1} = \dfrac{-3 - (-1)}{9 - 5}$

watch out for the double minus

$= \dfrac{-3 + 1}{4} = \dfrac{-2}{4} = -\dfrac{1}{2}$

Triangle abc is right-angled, since $m_1 \times m_2 = -1$

$2\left(-\dfrac{1}{2}\right) = -1$

(ii) A fact is that if a triangle is right-angled, then the centre of the circle that passes through the 3 vertices is the midpoint of the hypotenuse.

What does this mean in plain English? Well, to figure it out draw a rough diagram of a right-angled triangle.

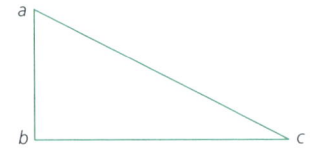

Since the triangle is right-angled at b, then the length ac is called the hypotenuse (furthest away from b). Then the centre of our circle is going to be the midpoint of ac and the radius is the distance from the centre to any of the vertices. This is a piece of information that you just learn; you do not have to know why or where it has come from.

(a) Centre = midpoint between the points (7, 3) and (9, –3)

Centre = (8, 0)

(b) Radius = distance from centre (8, 0) to either point (7, 3) = $\sqrt{10}$

(c) Use general equation

$(x - h)^2 + (y - k)^2 = r^2$
Centre $(h, k) = (8, 0)$ and radius $r = \sqrt{10}$

$(x - 8)^2 + (y - 0)^2 = 10$

$(x - 8)^2 + y^2 = 10$

To find the image of a circle under a transformation

Radius will stay the same; only have to transform the centre.

Step 1: Find the centre and radius.
Step 2: Use transformation to get new centre.
Step 3: Find new circle, using new centre and keeping old radius and formula $(x - h)^2 + (y - k)^2 = r^2$.

Example: Find the image of $(x - 3)^2 + (y + 5)^2 = 36$ under the transformation (1, 2) to (3, –4).

Solution

Centre (3, –5)   Radius = 6

Transformation (1, 2) to (3, –4). What has happened to the values of x and the values of y?

The x-value has gone from 1 to 3, so it has gone up in value by +2.

The y-value has gone from 2 to –4, so it has gone down in value by –6.

We can make a rule for this translation: $x + 2$, $y - 6$ and apply this rule to the point we must move.

Centre (3, –5) will move to (5, –11), since $3 + 2 = 5$ and $-5 - 6 = -11$.

Use new centre (5, –11) and radius = 6 in equation $(x - h)^2 + (y - k)^2 = r^2$ to get

$(x - 5)^2 + (y + 11)^2 = 36$.

103

Chapter 10
Theorems and Enlargements

Contents

(a) Theorems (page 104)
(b) Theorem Use (page 108)
(c) Enlargements (page 109).

There are only 10 theorems that you must be able to prove.

To learn the theorem

→ Write each one out in your handbook copy nice and neatly.
→ The next night, see whether you can write out one of them.
→ Leave for a few days and then see whether you can write out without notes.

Theorem 1

The sum of the measures of the angles of a triangle is 180°.

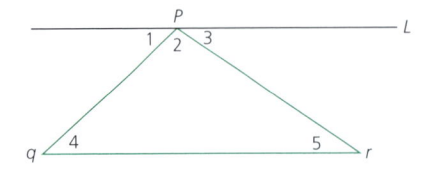

Proof: Draw $L \parallel qr$

$\angle 1 + \angle 2 + \angle 3 = 180°$ straight line

$\angle 1 = \angle 4$ alternate

$\angle 3 = \angle 5$ alternate

Substitute $\angle 4$ for $\angle 1$ and $\angle 5$ for $\angle 3$

$\angle 4 + \angle 2 + \angle 5 = 180°$

Corollary 1

An exterior angle of a triangle is equal in measure to the sum of the measures of the two remote interior angles.

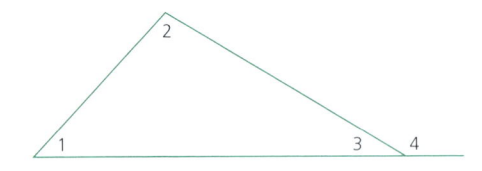

Proof: $\angle 1 + \angle 2 + \angle 3 = 180°$

(angles of a triangle)

$\angle 3 + \angle 4 = 180°$

(straight line)

$\angle 1 + \angle 2 + \angle 3 = \angle 3 + \angle 4$

(both 180°)

$\angle 1 + \angle 2 = \angle 4$

(cancel $\angle 3$ both sides)

Corollary 2

An exterior angle of a triangle is greater than either of the remote interior angles.

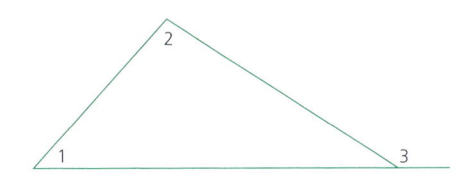

Proof: ∠3 = ∠1 + ∠2 exterior angle

∠1 > 0   and   ∠2 > 0

∠3 > ∠1   and   ∠3 > ∠2

Theorem 2

Opposite sides of a parallelogram have equal lengths.

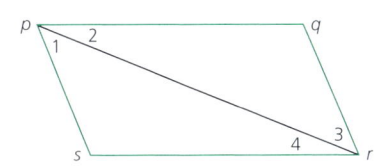

Proof: In △pqr and △psr

∠1 = ∠3   alternate

∠2 = ∠4   alternate

|pr| = |pr| common

△pqr is congruent to △psr ASA

|ps| = |qr| corresponding

|pq| = |sr| corresponding

Theorem 3

If 3 parallel lines make intercepts of equal length on a transversal, then they will also make intercepts of equal length on any other tranversal.

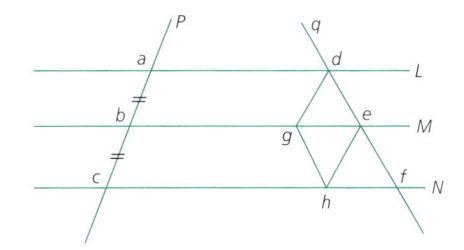

Construction: Complete parallelograms *adgb* and *dehg*.

Proof:

dehg is a parallelogram

so |gh| = |de| opposite sides

gh ∥ ef   construction

and   M ∥ N   given

so   *efhg* is a parallelogram

so |gh| = |ef| opposite sides

so |de| = |ef|

Theorem 4

A line that is parallel to one side of a triangle, and that cuts a second side, will cut the third side in the same proportion as the second.

Proof: Let x divide $[pq]$ in the ratio $m : n$,

so $\dfrac{|px|}{|xq|} = \dfrac{m}{n}$

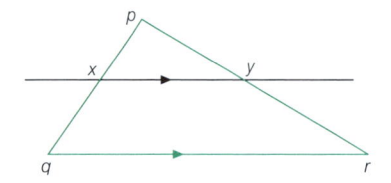

Divide [px] into m equal part.

Divide [xq] into n equal parts.

Through each point thus obtained on [px] and [xq], draw lines parallel to qr to meet pr.

So [pr] is divided into m equal parts and [yr] is divided into n equal parts

$$\Rightarrow \quad \frac{|py|}{|yr|} = \frac{m}{n} = \frac{|px|}{|xq|}.$$

Theorem 5

If the 3 angles of one triangle have degree measures equal, respectively, to the degree measures of the angles of a second triangle, then the lengths of the corresponding sides of the two triangles are proportional.

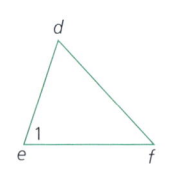

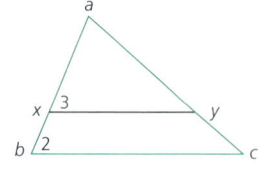

Construction: Let $\triangle axy$ be the image of $\triangle def$ under a translation.

Proof

$$\angle 1 = \angle 2 \quad \text{given}$$
and $\quad \angle 1 = \angle 3 \quad$ same angle
$$\therefore \quad \angle 2 = \angle 3$$

$$\therefore \quad xy \parallel bc$$

$$\therefore \quad \frac{|ab|}{|ax|} = \frac{|ac|}{|ay|}$$

$$\Rightarrow \quad \frac{|ab|}{|de|} = \frac{|ac|}{|df|}$$

Similarly, $\quad \frac{|ab|}{|de|} = \frac{|bc|}{|ef|}$

$$\therefore \quad \frac{|ab|}{|de|} = \frac{|ac|}{|df|} = \frac{|bc|}{|ef|}$$

Theorem 6

In a right-angled triangle, the square of the length of the side opposite to the right angle is equal to the sum of the squares of the lengths of the other two sides.

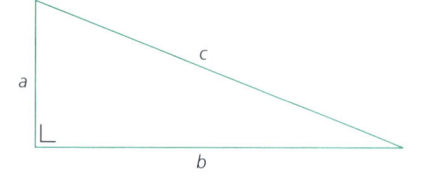

Construction: Construct a square using four congruent right-angled triangles.

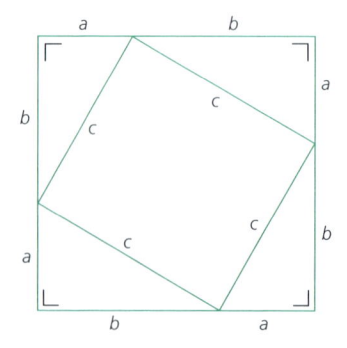

Proof: Area of larger square
$= (a + b)^2 = 4$ (area of one triangle) $+ c^2$

$\Rightarrow \quad (a+b)^2 = 4\left(\frac{1}{2}ab\right) + c^2$

$\Rightarrow \quad a^2 + 2ab + b^2 = 2ab + c^2$

$\Rightarrow \quad a^2 + b^2 = c^2$

Theorem 7

If the square of the length of one side of a triangle is equal to the sum of the squares of the lengths of the other two sides, then the triangle has a right angle, and this is opposite the longest side.

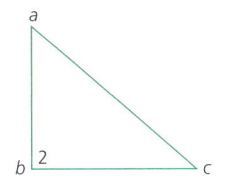

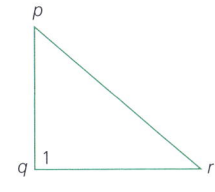

Construction:

Draw $\triangle pqr$ such that $\angle 1 = 90°$ and $|pq| = |ab|$ and $|qr| = |bc|$.

Proof:

$|ab|^2 + |bc|^2 = |ac|^2$ given

but $|pq|^2 + |qr|^2 = |pr|^2$ as $\angle 1 = 90°$

so $|pr| = |ac|$

$\therefore \triangle abc = \triangle pqr$ SSS

$\therefore \angle 2 = \angle 1 = 90°$ corresponding angles

$\angle abc$ is a right angle and is opposite the longest side.

Theorem 8

The products of the lengths of the sides of a triangle by the corresponding altitudes are equal.

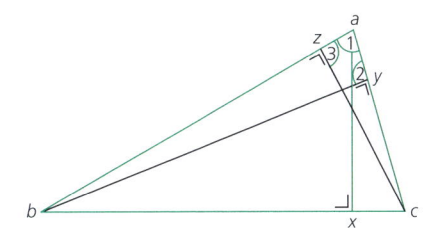

Proof

In $\triangle$s *aby* and *acz*:

$\angle 1 = \angle 1$ common angle

$\angle 2 = \angle 3 = 90°$ given

So $\triangle$s *aby* and *acz* are equiangular and corresponding sides are in proportion

$\therefore \quad \dfrac{|ab|}{|ac|} = \dfrac{|by|}{|cz|}$

cross-multiply

$\therefore \quad |ab|.|cz| = |ac|.|by|$

Similarly, $|ab|.|cz| = |bc|.|ax|$

$\therefore \quad |ab|.|cz| = |ac|.|by| = |bc|.|ax|$

Theorem 9

If the lengths of two sides of a triangle are unequal, then the degree measures of the angles opposite to them are unequal, with the greater angle opposite the longer side.

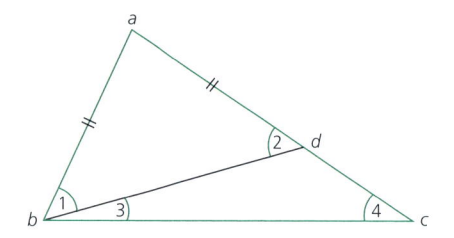

Construction:

Join b to d such that $|ab| = |ad|$.

Proof:

In $\triangle abd$:

$\qquad |ab| = |ad| \qquad$ construction

so $\quad \angle 1 = \angle 2$

In $\triangle bcd$,

$\qquad \angle 2 > \angle 4 \qquad$ exterior angle

$\therefore \quad \angle 1 > \angle 4$

$\therefore \quad \angle 1 + \angle 3 > \angle 4$

$\therefore \quad \angle abc > \angle acb$

Theorem 10

The sum of the lengths of any two sides of a triangle is greater than that of the third side.

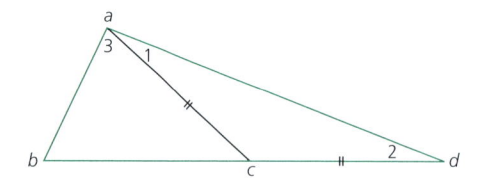

Construction:

Join c to d such that $|ac| = |cd|$.

Proof:

In $\triangle acd$:

$\qquad |ac| = |cd| \qquad$ construction

so $\qquad |\angle 1| = |\angle 2|$

$\therefore \quad |\angle 1| + |\angle 3| > |\angle 2|$

$\therefore \qquad |bd| > |ab|$

side opposite greater angle

but $\qquad |bd| = |bc| + |cd|$

$\qquad \qquad = |bc| + |ac|$

$\therefore \quad |bc| + |ac| > |ab|$

Theorem Use

Most of the questions they have asked here have been very easy.

Even if you do not know how to prove the theorems, you could try these parts.

Method

Draw the diagram for yourself and fill in as much information as you can. You need to know what the theorems say.

Example: In the diagram, $|ab| = |ac|$ and $|\angle bad| = 102°$.

(i) Find $|\angle cab|$.
(ii) Find $|\angle abc|$.

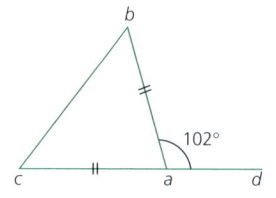

Solution

$A = 180° - 102°$

$\quad = 78°$

108

angle on a straight line

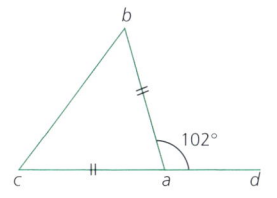

Since this is an isosceles triangle, the other 2 angles must be equal

$$180 - 78 = 102 \div 2 = 51°.$$

Example: In the triangle abc, $|ad| = |bd|$, $|\angle abd| = |\angle dbc|$ and $|\angle dab| = 48°$.

Find $|\angle dcb|$.

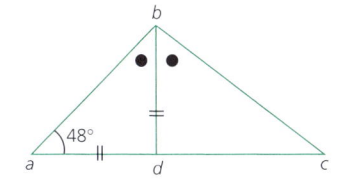

Solution

must be 48° since base angles of isosceles triangle are equal

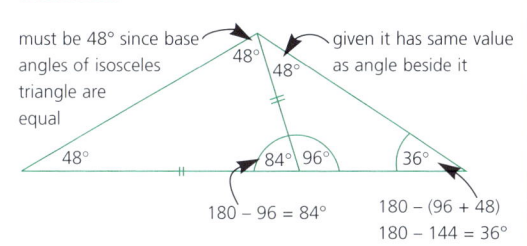

48°   48°   48°
84° 96°   36°

$180 - 96 = 84°$
$180 - (96 + 48)$
$180 - 144 = 36°$

given it has same value as angle beside it

Example: Find the area of triangle abc if $|\angle abc| = 90°$, $|ac| = 26$ and $|bc| = 10$.

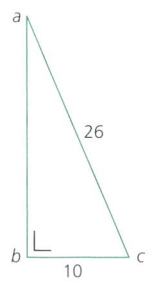

Solution

Let the unknown side be x.

Since it is right-angled and we have 2 lengths, then we use Pythagoras' theorem:

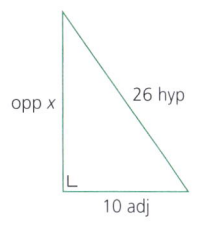

$$H^2 = A^2 + O^2$$

fill in $H = 26$, $A = 10$ and $O = x$

$$26^2 = 10^2 + x^2$$

square out

$$676 = x^2 + 100$$

bring 100 to other side

$$576 = x^2$$

swap sides

$$x^2 = 576$$

to get rid of square find square root

$$x = 24$$

$$\text{Area} = \frac{1}{2} \text{ base} \times \text{perpendicular height}$$

$$= \frac{1}{2} \cdot 10 \times 24 = 120 \text{ sq. units}$$

Enlargements

The idea here is that a shape is either enlarged or reduced by a set amount called a scale factor, k.

If the size of an object doubles, then $k = 2$.

To find *k* we have 2 different types of question:

If they give us 2 lengths, we can find *k*.

$$k = \frac{\text{length of image side}}{\text{length of original side}}$$

If we are given 2 areas:

$$k^2 = \frac{\text{Area of image shape}}{\text{Area of original shape}}$$

Example: The triangle *xzy* is the image of the triangle *dgh* under the enlargement, centre *o*, with |*dg*| = 8, |*xz*| = 12 and |*xy*| = 9.

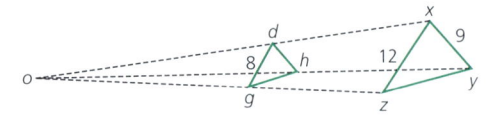

(i) Find the scale factor of the enlargement.
(ii) Find |*dh*|.
(iii) The area of the triangle *xzy* is 27 square units. Find the area of the triangle *dgh*.

Solution

(i) We need to find lengths in each triangle that correspond.
|*dg*| = 8 corresponds to |*xz*| = 12. △*xyz* is the image of △*dhg*

$$k = \frac{12}{8} = 1.5$$

(ii) |*xy*| = 9, but |*dh*| is its corresponding length which has been reduced.

$$|dh| = \frac{9}{1.5} = 6$$

> When a side has been reduced we *divide by k*.
> When a side has been increased we *multiply by k*.

(iii) Area △*xzy* = 27, but △*dgh* is a reduced area.

Area at △*dgh* = $\frac{27}{(1.5)^2}$

$$= \frac{27}{2.25} = 12$$

> When an area has been reduced we *divide by k²*.
> When an area has been increased we *multiply by k²*.

Example: The triangle *odc* is the image of the triangle *oab* under an enlargement, centre *o*. |*cd*| = 9 and |*ab*| = 15.

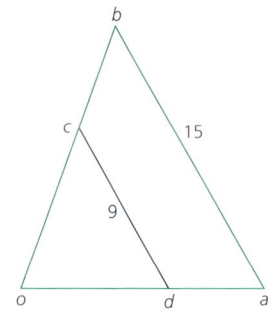

(i) Find the scale factor of the enlargement.
(ii) If the area of triangle *oab* is 87.5 square units, find the area of triangle *odc*.
(iii) Write down the area of the region *abcd*.

Solution

(i) $k = \frac{15}{9} = \frac{5}{3}$

(ii) Area of △*odc* = $\frac{\text{Area of } \triangle oab}{k^2}$

$$= \frac{87.5}{\left(\frac{5}{3}\right)^2} = 31.5$$

(iii) Area of region *abcd*
 = Area of △*oab* − Area of △*ocd*
 = 87.5 − 31.5
 = 56 sq. units

Chapter 11
Trigonometry

Contents

(a) Measure of angles (page 111)
(b) Use of the calculator (page 111)
(c) Unit circle (page 112)
(d) Solving triangles (page 113)
(e) Compound angles (page 123).

Measure of angles

There are two ways of measuring angles.

Degrees: There are 360° in a circle.
Radian : π radians = 180°

$$\pi = 180°$$

Note: Radian measure will always contain π and therefore there is no symbol for rads.

Example: Convert 60° to radians.

Solution

$$180° = \pi$$

$$1° = \frac{\pi}{180}$$

$$60° = \frac{60\pi}{180} = \frac{\pi}{3}$$

Example: Convert $\frac{\pi}{2}$ to degrees.

Solution

$$\pi = 180°$$

$$\frac{\pi}{2} = \frac{180}{2}$$

$$= 90°$$

Use of the calculator

Turn on the calculator.
Make sure the calculator says deg (or D).

Type 1

To find the sin, cos or tan of a given angle

Example: Find sin 31° to two decimal places.

Solution

Turn on calculator, hit $\boxed{\sin}$, then 31, then $\boxed{=}$

$$\sin 31° = 0.515038074$$

To round to *two* decimal places look at the *third* digit after the decimal point. If this digit is 4 or less we leave alone, if 5 or more we round up.

$\sin 31° = 0.52$ since the third digit was 5 we round from 0.515 to 0.52

Example: Find cos 54° 29′ to 2 decimal places.

Solution

Turn on the calculator. Hit [cos], then 54, then [DMS], then 29, then [=]

$$\cos 54°29' = 0.5809$$
$$= 0.58$$

Note: The [DMS] button on some calculators is shown as [″′]

Type 2

To find the angle given the value of sin, cos or tan

Example: If tan A = 1.23, find a value for A.

Solution

Turn on the calculator. Hit [2nd], then [tan], then 1.23[=]

$$\tan A = 1.23$$
$$A = 50.88°$$

If the question says to write answer to nearest one degree, then answer is 51°.

If the question says to write answer to nearest one minute, then we hit [2nd], then [DMS] to get 51°53′.

Unit circle

To find whether an angle is positive or negative, remember **All Silly Tom Cats**

Sin	All
Tan	Cos

Example: Express in surd form: sin 135°.

Solution

Two parts that we must deal with which stem from the angle given, which in this case is 135°:

Part 1: Figure out whether the answer is positive or negative by using All Silly Tom Cats.

Part 2: Figure out the equivalent angle in the first quadrant by using the idea below.

Put the two parts together and we can use the maths tables, page 9, to come up with the answer.

If B is the angle we are given and A is the required angle in the first quadrant:	
$A = 180° - B$	$A = B$
$A = B - 180°$	$A = 360° - B$

135° is in the second quadrant where sin is positive, so the answer will be positive.

The angle in the first quadrant comes from 180° − 135° = 45°

$$\sin 135° = \sin 45° = \frac{1}{\sqrt{2}}$$

Note: $45° = \frac{\pi}{4}$, so that in the maths tables, page 9, we look in the box. Go across the top until we come to $\frac{\pi}{4}$, down to the sin line, so that we come up with the answer of $\frac{1}{\sqrt{2}}$.

Equations

This works backwards from what we have just done, and there are slightly different rules to learn.

Example: Solve $\sin A = -\frac{\sqrt{3}}{2}$, where $0 \leq A \leq 360°$.

Solution

There are three steps to follow to find the answers.

Step 1: Use the sign given to decide which quadrants we are in.
Step 2: Drop the sign and use the tables, page 9, to find the angle in the first quadrant.
Step 3: Use the rules below to figure out the required answers.

If A is the angle in the first quadrant then the required angle B in other quadrants is found from:	
$B = 180° - A$	$B = A$
$B = 180° + A$	$B = 360° - A$

From All Silly Tom Cats we know that the answers to this question are in the 3rd and 4th quadrants.

$\sin A = \frac{\sqrt{3}}{2}$ find angle in first quadrant

$A = 60°$

Answers: $A = 240°$ or $A = 300°$

Example: Solve the equation $A = -1$, where $0° \leq A \leq 360°$.

Solution

From All Silly Tom Cats we know that the answers to this question are in the 2nd and 4th quadrants.

$\tan A = 1$ find angle in first quadrant

$A = 45°$

Answers: $A = 135°$ or $A = 315°$

Solving triangles

This is by far the most important part of this chapter. No matter what type of question we are asked, it comes down to either a right-angled or a non-right-angled triangle.

Try to use the following method.

Step 1: Read the question (several times).
Step 2: Draw out a diagram for yourself and FILL IN as much information as possible.
Step 3: Ask the simple question: '**Is it right-angled?**'
If the answer is **YES**, then use sin, cos or tan, or Pythagoras' theorem.
If the answer is **NO**, then use sine rule, cosine rule or area.

Right-angled triangles

Need only two pieces of information to be able to find a third, using:

(a) Silly Old Harry Caught A Herring Trawling Off America
(b) Pythagoras' theorem.

113

Non-right-angled triangles

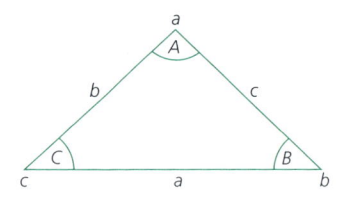

Formula 1. Area of a triangle – used to find:

(i) area of a triangle given two lengths and included angle
(ii) length or angle given area

Formula 2. Sine Rule – used to find length or angle. We must be given at least one angle and the length opposite.

Formula 3. Cosine Rule – used to find one length, given two lengths and included angle.

Note: All the above formulae are in the maths tables, so find them now – do not learn them.

Note: You should know that the angles in a triangle sum to 180°.

Words of importance

Horizontal: lying flat on the ground

Vertical: standing straight up

Angle of elevation: the angle through which we look up to the sky from the ground (horizontal)

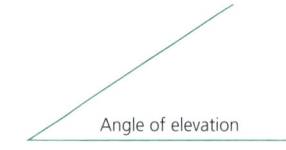

Angle of depression: angle through which we look down from top of a cliff face

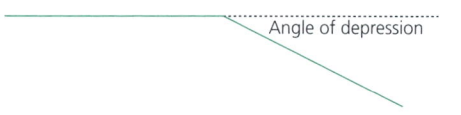

Direction: north, south, east or west

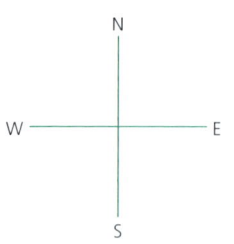

There are 4 types of question that we can be asked to solve:

➢ right-angled triangle
➢ area of a triangle and a sector
➢ non-right-angled triangles
➢ double triangles.

Right-angled triangles

We are going to be dealing with a right-angled triangle, which has three important sides called:

(a) the hypotenuse (always opposite the right angle)
(b) the opposite (away from the angle)
(c) the adjacent (beside the right angle).

The first thing that you will do in any question is DRAW a diagram and mark in each of the above lines.

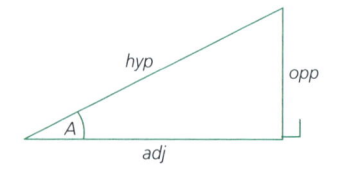

sin, cos and tan

Silly Old Harry Caught A Herring Trawling Off America

$$\sin A = \frac{opp}{hyp}$$
$$\cos A = \frac{adj}{hyp}$$
$$\tan A = \frac{opp}{adj}$$

Given two lengths, to find the third length

Here we need a different formula called Pythagoras' theorem, which says that the square on the hyp is equal to the sum of the squares on the other two sides.

$$H^2 = A^2 + O^2$$

Example: Use the information given in the diagram to show that

$$\sin^2 \vartheta + \cos^2 \vartheta > \tan^2 \vartheta$$

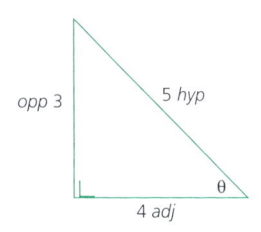

(triangle with opp 3, hyp 5, adj 4, angle θ)

Solution

$$\sin \vartheta = \frac{opp}{hyp} = \frac{3}{5}$$
$$\cos \vartheta = \frac{adj}{hyp} = \frac{4}{5}$$
$$\tan \vartheta = \frac{opp}{adj} = \frac{3}{4}$$

Note: $\sin^2 \vartheta = (\sin \vartheta)^2$ means find $\sin \vartheta$ and then square it.

Note: ϑ (Greek *theta*) is sometimes used instead of A, but both just stand for an angle.

$$\sin^2 \vartheta + \cos^2 \vartheta > \tan^2 \vartheta$$
$$\left(\frac{3}{5}\right)^2 + \left(\frac{4}{5}\right)^2 > \left(\frac{3}{4}\right)^2$$
$$\frac{9}{25} + \frac{16}{25} > \frac{9}{16}$$
$$1 > \frac{9}{16}$$

Example: If $\sin A = {}^5/_{13}$ and A is an acute angle, write down the value of $\cos A$ without tables or calculator.

Solution

(a) Draw a diagram.
(b) Fill in as much information as possible.

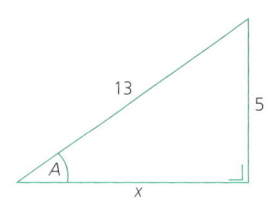

(triangle with hypotenuse 13, opposite side 5, angle A, adjacent side x)

$$\sin A = \frac{5}{13} = \frac{opp}{hyp}.$$

We draw a right-angled triangle and mark in the angle A. The length opposite the angle is 5 and the *hyp* is 13. We call the other side x and use Pythagoras' theorem to find the value of x.

$$H^2 = A^2 + O^2$$
$$13^2 = x^2 + 5^2$$
$$169 = x^2 + 25$$
$$144 = x^2$$
$$12 = x$$
$$\cos A = \frac{12}{13}$$

115

Note: 'Without tables or calculator' does not exclude page 9, which we can always use.

Example: Find the length of the sides of a square, which has a diagonal of length 10 cm.

Solution

The first thing to do is draw a diagram.

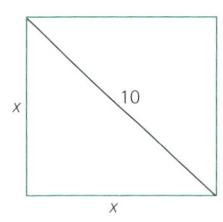

Here we have two right-angled triangles with $hyp = 10$
$adj = x$
$opp = x$

$$H^2 = A^2 + O^2$$

sub in lengths of sides

$$10^2 = x^2 + x^2$$

add $x^2 + x^2 = 2x^2$

$$100 = 2x^2$$

swap sides to have letters on left

$$2x^2 = 100$$

divide across by 2

$$x^2 = 50$$

to get rid of square, take square root

$$x = \sqrt{50}$$

Example: Find the value of x.

Question:

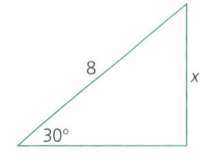

Solution

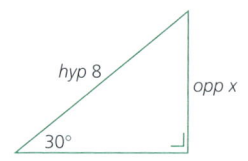

$$\sin A = \frac{opp}{hyp}, \quad \cos A = \frac{adj}{hyp}, \quad \tan A = \frac{opp}{adj}$$

Which of the three can we use in this question?

We have the angle and the *hyp*, but need the *opp*.

Which one has *hyp* and *opp* in it? The answer is sin.

We use $\sin A = \frac{opp}{hyp}$ and replace $A = 30$, $opp = x$ and $hyp = 8$.

$$\sin A = \frac{opp}{hyp}$$

sub in the figures

$$\sin 30 = \frac{x}{8}$$

find sin 30 using calculator

$$0.5 = \frac{x}{8}$$

cross-multiply

$$8(0.5) = x$$

$$x = 4$$

Note: If you write down what sin, cos and tan are, you will get at least attempt marks.

Note: In many of the questions it is much harder to see what we are asked to find, because of the way the question is phrased.

Example: A ladder which is 6 m long leans against a vertical wall. The foot of the ladder is on level ground at a distance of 1 m from the bottom of the wall. Find the measure of the angle that the ladder makes with the ground, to the nearest degree.

Solution

You have to draw a diagram for the information that we are given.

Since it is a vertical wall and horizontal ground, then there must be a right angle across which the ladder lies.

Draw out the triangle and mark in two sides:

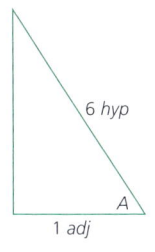

$hyp = 6$ and $adj = 1$.

Now have to decide whether we use sin, cos or tan.

Since we have *adj* and *hyp*, we will use cos.

$$\cos A = \frac{adj}{hyp}$$

replace $adj = 1$ and $hyp = 6$ to find angle A

$$\cos A = \frac{1}{6}$$

on calculator hit [2nd], then [cos], then 1 [$a^b/_c$] 6 [=]

$$A = 80°$$

Example: A man stands on top of a vertical cliff. He spots a buoy 27 m from the base of the cliff at an angle of depression of 25°. How high is the cliff, to two decimal places?

Solution

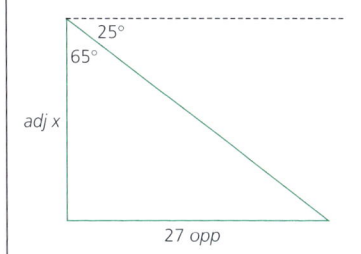

We know the angle of depression is 25°, so the angle beside it (inside our right angle) is 65°.

Since we have the *opp* length and need the *adj*, we will use tan.

$$\tan A = \frac{opp}{adj}$$

replace $opp = 27$ and $A = 65$ to find *adj*

$$\tan 65 = \frac{27}{x}$$

$$2.1445 = \frac{27}{x}$$

cross-multiply

$$2.1445\, x = 27$$

$$x = \frac{27}{2.1445}$$

$$x = 12.59 \text{ m}$$

117

Area of a triangle and a sector

Example: Find the area of the triangle shown:

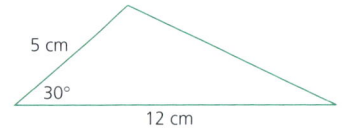

Solution

Area of a triangle = $\frac{1}{2} ab \sin C$, which means we multiply one length by another and by sin of the angle between the two lengths.

$$\text{Area} = \frac{1}{2} ab \sin C$$

sub in $a = 5$, $b = 12$ and $C = 30°$

$$= \frac{1}{2}(5)(12) \sin 30$$

use the calculator to find sin 30

$$= (0.5)(5)(12)(0.5)$$

change $\frac{1}{2}$ to 0.5 and use calculator to multiply out

$$= 15 \text{ cm}$$

Example: The area of the triangle pqr is 9028 m², $|pq| = 200$ m and $|pqr| = 47°44'$. Find $|qr|$.

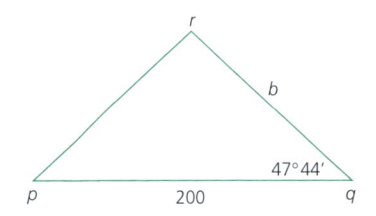

Solution

$$\text{Area} = \frac{1}{2} ab \sin C$$

sub in $a = 200$, $b = b$ and $C = 47° 44'$

$$9028 = \frac{1}{2}(200)(b) \sin 47°44'$$

use the calculator to find sin 47°44'

$$9028 = (0.5)(200)(b)(0.74)$$

multiply out the right-hand side

$$9028 = 74b$$

swap sides and solve

$$74b = 9028$$
$$b = 122 \text{ m}$$

Sector of a circle

The best way to do this is not to use any trigonometry, but to use the methods from the area and volume section.

Make a fraction by using: $\dfrac{\text{given angle}}{360}$

Example: In the diagram, o is the centre of a sector opq which has a radius 5 cm. $|\angle poq| = 80°$.

Find, correct to two decimal places:

(i) area of triangle poq
(ii) the area of the shaded region, taking $\pi = 3.14$.

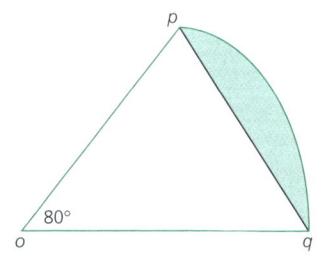

Solution

(i) Find the area of triangle opq

$$\text{Area} = \frac{1}{2} ab \sin C$$

118

sub in $a = 5$, $b = 5$ and $C = 80°$

$$= \frac{1}{2}(5)(5) \sin 80$$

use the calculator to find sin 80

$$= (0.5)(5)(5)(0.9848)$$

change $\frac{1}{2}$ to 0.5 and use calculator to multiply out

$$= 12.31 \text{ cm}^2$$

(ii) Area of shaded region = area of sector opq – area of triangle opq

Find the area of a full circle and then decide what fraction of a circle we have.

Circle: $r = 5$, $\pi = 3.14$; find A.

$$\text{Area} = \pi r^2$$
$$= 3.14(5)^2$$

square first, then multiply

$$= 3.14(25)$$
$$= 78.5$$

$$80° = \frac{80}{360} = \frac{2}{9}$$

on a calculator put in 80 $\boxed{a^b/c}$ 360 $\boxed{=}$ and it will say 2 r 9

$$\text{Sector } \frac{2}{9}(78.5) = 17.444$$
$$= 17.44$$

to 2 decimal places

Shaded area = 17.44 – 12.31 = 5.13 cm²

Non-right-angled triangles

Sine rule

Example: Two lighthouses, p and q, are 73 km apart; q is directly East of p. Another lighthouse, r, is situated 52 km from q. The bearing of r from p is E 32°20′ N. Calculate $|pr|$, correct to the nearest kilometre.

Solution

This is an example of a direction question. Most of the time they will draw the diagram that goes with the question. You should try to see whether you can draw the diagram from the given information without looking at the following diagram.

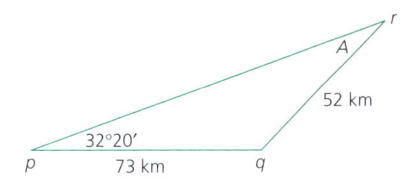

Is the triangle right-angled? No, so you must move on.

Have we an angle and its opposite length, so that we can use the sine rule? Yes.

The next question is what can we find? We have the length $|qr|$ and its opposite angle and we have the length $|pq|$ so we can find its opposite angle, which is marked in the diagram as the angle A.

This is the rule in the maths tables

$$\frac{A}{\sin A} = \frac{b}{\sin B}$$

119

put the figures in

$$\frac{73}{\sin A} = \frac{52}{\sin 32°20'}$$

cross-multiply

$$73 \sin 32°20' = 52 \sin A$$

find sin 32°20' using the calculator

$$73(0.5348) = 52 \sin A$$

swap both sides and divide across by 52

$$52 \sin A = 39.04$$

$$\sin A = \frac{39.04}{52}$$

divide bottom into top

$$\sin A = 0.7508$$

use the calculator to find the angle

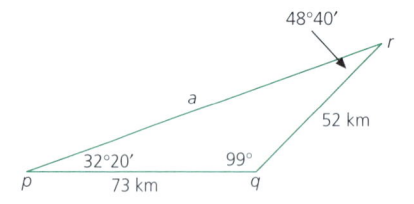

$$A = 48.66°$$

$$A = 48°40'$$

Add 32°20' + 48°40'; now we can find the third angle.

$$180° - 81° = 99°$$

Use the sine rule again to find |pr|, which we will call a.

$$\frac{a}{\sin A} = \frac{b}{\sin B}$$

$$\frac{a}{\sin 99°} = \frac{52}{\sin 32°20'}$$

$$\frac{a}{0.9877} = \frac{52}{0.5348}$$

$$0.5348a = 52(0.9877)$$

$$0.5348a = 51.36$$

$$a = \frac{51.35}{0.5348} = 96.04$$

$$= 96 \text{ to the nearest km.}$$

Cosine rule

Example: One side of a triangle has a length of 4 cm and another has a length of 7 cm. The angle between these two sides measures 60°. Find the length of the third side.

Solution

First thing to do is to draw a triangle for the above information and call the missing side a. The reason to name the missing side is that both the sine rule and cosine rule start with a.

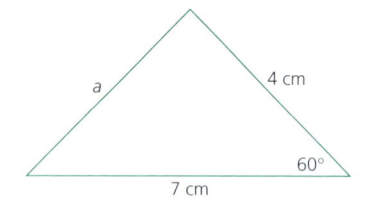

Is the triangle right-angled? No, so you must move on.

Have we an angle and its opposite length so that we can use the sine rule? No, so move on.

We are left with no other option but to use the cosine rule.

$$a^2 = b^2 + c^2 - 2bc \cos A$$

In this question $a = a$, $b = 4$, $c = 7$ and $A = 60°$.

Note: It does not matter which side we call b and which we call c.

$a^2 = b^2 + c^2 - 2bc \cos A$

sub in the figures

$a^2 = 4^2 + 7^2 - 2(4)(7) \cos 60$

find cos 60°

$a^2 = 16 + 49 - 56(0.5)$

take your time; square first and multiply

$a^2 = 16 + 49 - 28$

$a^2 = 37$

$a = \sqrt{37}$ cm

Double triangles

Example: *abc* is a triangle and $d \in [bc]$, as shown. If $|bd| = 4$ cm, $|ac| = 6$ cm, $|\angle acd| = 65°$ and $|\angle dac| = 70°$, find:

(i) $|ad|$, correct to the nearest cm
(ii) $|ab|$, correct to the nearest cm.

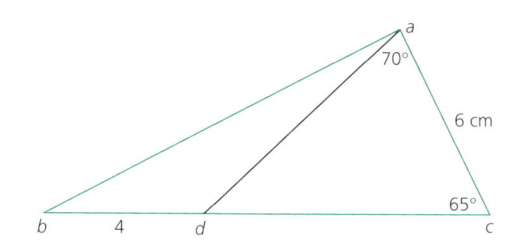

Solution

How many triangles are in the diagram?

The answer is that there are 3 triangles, which you could draw out. We will draw out the triangles that have at least one length in them and hope that in one of them we will be able to use the sine rule or cosine rule.

Note: When we draw out the triangles for ourselves we do not have to draw a perfect replica, just a rough idea.

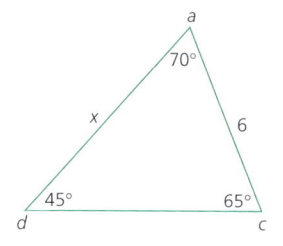

Mark in the angle at $d = 180 - (65 + 70) = 45°$

Is the triangle right-angled? No, so you must move on.

Have we an angle and its opposite length so that we can use the sine rule? Yes.

$$\frac{a}{\sin A} = \frac{b}{\sin B}$$

$$\frac{x}{\sin 65°} = \frac{6}{\sin 45°}$$

$$\frac{x}{0.9063} = \frac{6}{0.7071}$$

$0.7071x = 6(0.9063)$

$0.7071x = 5.4378$

$$x = \frac{5.4378}{0.7071} = 7.69$$

$x = 8$ to the nearest cm.

Fill in as much information as you can on the main diagram.

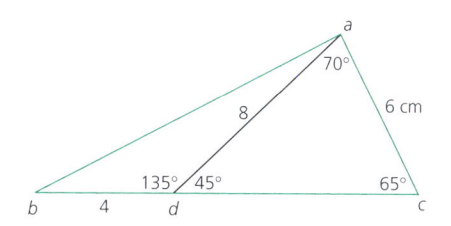

Which triangle will we draw out to try to come up with $|ab|$?

121

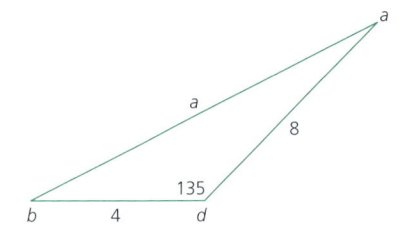

Since we have two lengths and the included angle, we can find the third length by using the cosine rule.

$$a^2 = b^2 + c^2 - 2bc \cos A$$

In this question $a = a$, $b = 8$, $c = 4$ and $A = 135°$.

$$a^2 = b^2 + c^2 - 2bc \cos A$$
$$a^2 = 8^2 + 4^2 - 2(8)(4) \cos 135°$$
$$a^2 = 64 + 16 - 64(-0.7071)$$
$$a^2 = 64 + 16 + 45.25$$
$$a^2 = 125.25$$
$$a = \sqrt{125.25} = 11.19 = 11 \text{ cm}$$

Example: t, x, u and y are points on level ground, x, u and y being in a straight line.
From x the direction of t is East 39°46′ North.
From y the direction of t is West 68°26′ North.
u is directly South of t.
$|xy| = 95$ m
Find $|tu|$, correct to the nearest metre.

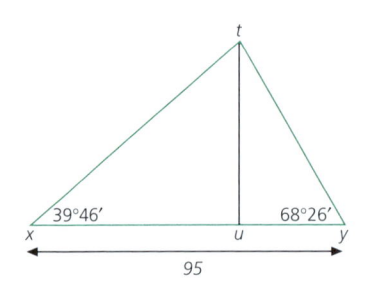

Solution

East 39°46′ North means go right and then up.
West 68°26′ North means go left and then up.

Again there are 3 possible triangles for us to draw out, but the question is: which one has got a length in it?

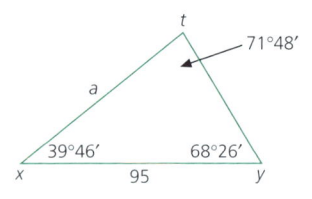

Add 39°46′ + 68°26′ = 108°12′; now we can find the third angle.

180° − 108°12′ = 71°48′; the best way to do this on a calculator is to put in 180 [DMS] 00 − 108 [DMS] 12.

Is the triangle right-angled? No, so you must move on.

Have we an angle and its opposite length so that we can use the sine rule? Yes.

Mark in missing side $|tx|$ as a and continue as above.

$$\frac{a}{\sin A} = \frac{b}{\sin B}$$

$$\frac{a}{\sin 68°26′} = \frac{95}{\sin 71°48′}$$

$$\frac{a}{0.9299} = \frac{95}{0.9499}$$

$$0.9499a = 95(0.9299)$$

$$0.9499a = 88.349$$

$$a = \frac{88.349}{0.9499} = 93 \text{ m}$$

to the nearest metre

$$\sin 39°46' = \frac{b}{93}$$

$$0.6396 = \frac{b}{93}$$

$$93(0.6396) = b$$

$$b = 59.48$$

$$b = 59 \text{ m}$$

to the nearest metre.

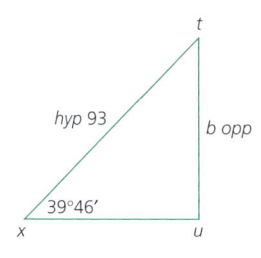

Compound angle formulae

Example: If $\cos A = \frac{3}{5}$ and $\sin B = \frac{12}{13}$ find $\cos (A + B)$.

Solution

$\cos (A + B) = \cos A \cos B - \sin A \sin B$. We must draw two triangles for the above two pieces of information.

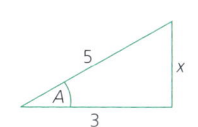

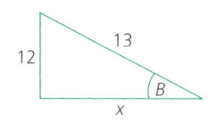

$$\cos A = \frac{3}{5} = \frac{adj}{hyp} \qquad \sin B = \frac{12}{13} = \frac{opp}{hyp}$$

$$x^2 + 3^2 = 5^2 \qquad x^2 + 12^2 = 13^2$$
$$x^2 + 9 = 25 \qquad x^2 + 144 = 169$$
$$x^2 = 16 \qquad x^2 = 25$$
$$x = 4 \qquad x = 5$$

$$\sin A = \frac{4}{5} \qquad \cos B = \frac{5}{13}$$

$$\cos (A + B) = \cos A \cos B - \sin A \sin B$$

$$= \left(\frac{3}{5}\right)\left(\frac{5}{13}\right) - \left(\frac{4}{5}\right)\left(\frac{12}{13}\right)$$

$$= \frac{15}{65} - \frac{48}{65}$$

$$= -\frac{33}{65}$$

Chapter 12
Probability

Contents

(a) Permutations (page 124)
(b) Selections or combinations (page 126)
(c) Basic Probability (page 128).

Permutations

There are three different types of question here:

(i) permutations of *n* objects *n* at a time
(ii) permutations of *n* objects taking *r* of them at a time
(iii) together.

> A permutation is an arrangement of a number of objects in a certain order.

Note: In answering this type of question **AND** means **MULTIPLY**; **OR** often means **ADD**.

Type 1

Permutations of *n* objects *n* at a time.

> If asked to arrange *n* objects, the answer is *n*! i.e. *n* factorial.

Example: In how many ways can 6 horses finish a race?

Solution

Answer is 6! = 720 ways.

Type 2

Permutation of *n* objects taking *r* of them at a time.

The easiest way to tackle these questions is to use spaces. In the first space fill in how many possible items could be in it, do the same for the second space and so on.

Example: How many three-digit numbers can be formed from 1, 2, 3, 4, each digit used only once?

(i) Write down the largest possible 3-digit number.
(ii) Write down the smallest possible number.
(iii) How many of these are over 300?
(iv) How many of these are odd?

Note: Question marks are very important here, and even though at first glance there seem to be four parts to this question, there is actually a fifth part at the start.

Solution

'Three-digit' means three spaces to fill with no restrictions.

There are 4 choices for the first place, but when this is filled there are only 3 possible digits for the next space and so on.

$$\underline{4} \times \underline{3} \times \underline{2} = 24$$

(i) Largest number is 432; start with biggest digit, then next biggest and next biggest.
(ii) Smallest number is 123; start with smallest.

Note: In a lot of questions a stipulation may be placed on one part; if this happens, read it carefully and see which space it affects.

(iii) 'Over 300' means that it must start with a 3 or 4, so that there are only 2 choices for the first space.

$$\underline{2} \times \underline{3} \times \underline{2} = 12$$

(iv) 'Odd' means that the last digit must be 1 or 3, so we have to fill the last space up first and then go back to the start and fill the first box. We have 2 choices for the last space, which when filled will leave 3 choices for the first space.

$$\underline{3} \times \underline{2} \times \underline{2} = 12$$

Example: How many three-digit numbers can be formed from 0, 1, 2, 3, each digit used only once?

Solution

The problem here is that a number cannot start with 0 unless it is stated in the question.

$$\underline{3} \times \underline{3} \times \underline{2} = 18$$

Example:
(i) How many different arrangements can be made using all the letters of the word *CARLOW*?
(ii) In how many ways can the 6 letters be arranged if they must end in a *W*?
(iii) How many permutations can be made if they must start with a vowel?

Solution

These questions can be done either using spaces, or the factorial *n*!

(i) 6 spaces to fill with 6 different letters.

$$\underline{6} \times \underline{5} \times \underline{4} \times \underline{3} \times \underline{2} \times \underline{1} = 720$$

(ii) If they end in a *W* we must fill the last space first, which has only one choice. The first space has then 5 choices, the second space has 4 choices and so on.

$$\underline{5} \times \underline{4} \times \underline{3} \times \underline{2} \times \underline{1} \times \underline{1} = 120$$

(iii) This time we look at the first space first. There are 2 choices: namely an *A* or *O*. The second space will then have 5 choices, the third space has 4 choices and so on.

$$\underline{2} \times \underline{5} \times \underline{4} \times \underline{3} \times \underline{2} \times \underline{1} = 240$$

Example: In how many ways can 4 boys and 3 girls be arranged in a line so that no two boys are together?

Solution

Must go *BGBGBGB*

$$\underline{4} \times \underline{3} \times \underline{3} \times \underline{2} \times \underline{2} \times \underline{1} \times \underline{1} = 144$$

Example: In how many ways can 4 boys and 4 girls be arranged in a line so that no two boys are together?

Solution

Must go *BGBGBGBG* but we must multiply by 2, because a boy could be first **or** a girl could be first.

$2(\underline{4} \times \underline{4} \times \underline{3} \times \underline{3} \times \underline{2} \times \underline{2} \times \underline{1} \times \underline{1}) = 1152$

Type 3

Together

This is where we have to arrange items in such a way as to keep two or more of them together. If we are supposed to keep two items together we treat the items we want together as one unit, but because they are not exactly the same we have to remember to multiply by 2.

Example: In how many ways can 5 boys stand side by side? If two of the boys are twins, in how many ways can the boys be arranged so that:

(i) the twins are together
(ii) the twins are not together?

Solution

5 boys can be arranged in 5! = 120 ways.

(i) The word 'together' leads to the very important idea of treating the twins as one unit and so arranging 4 units in total (3 individual boys and 1 set of twins), and then arranging the twins.

Twins together = 4! by 2! = 24 × 2
= 48 ways.

> Not together = total arrangement – the number of arrangements in which the objects are together.

(ii) Twins not together = 120 – 48 = 72 ways.

Example: In how many ways can *a*, *b*, *c*, *d*, *e* and *f* be arranged so that *a*, *b* and *c* are not together?

Solution

Not together = total – together

Total = 6! = 720

'Together' means *a*, *b*, *c* are treated as one unit. We must arrange the 4 units *abc*, *d*, *e* and *f*.

And within the four units we have to arrange *a*, *b*, *c*.

Together: 4! × 3! = 144

Answer = 720 – 144 = 576 ways.

Selections or combinations

Type 1

> In order to choose *r* objects from *n* we use:
>
> $$\binom{n}{r} = {}^nC_r$$

Example: In how many ways can 2 players be chosen from a group of 6?

Solution

$$\binom{6}{2} = 15$$

Note: On a calculator

$$\binom{6}{2} = 15 = 6 \boxed{\text{2nd F}} \boxed{5} \, 2 \, \boxed{=}$$

Type 2

Subdivide into 2 sections.

> When we have two different groups in the one question we make our choices from each group, and then multiply both results.

Example: An exam consists of two sections, section A and section B. Section A has 4 questions and section B has 5 questions. Each student must answer 5 questions in total. In how many ways can a student choose these 5 questions, given that she must answer at least two questions from each section?

Solution

Section A has 4 questions. Section B has 5 questions.

Must pick 5 questions, at least 2 from each section. What are the possible ways to do this?

Choose 2 from A and 3 from B **or** 3 from A and 2 from B.

2 from A and 3 from B

$$= \binom{4}{2} \times \binom{5}{3} = 6 \times 10 = 60$$

3 from A and 2 from B

$$= \binom{4}{3} \times \binom{5}{2} = 4 \times 10 = 40$$

No. of choices = 60 + 40 = 100.

Example: A delegation of four is to be chosen from a committee of 7 men and 4 women. How many delegations are possible if there must be:

(i) exactly 2 women?
(ii) at least 2 women?
(iii) at most 1 woman?

Note 1: 'Exactly' is easy to deal with, as it means that there is only one case to consider.

Note 2: 'At least' is much more difficult, as you must think out all the possible combinations and then figure each one out and add up all your answers. The same idea is followed when we see the phrase 'at most'.

Solution

(i) 'Exactly two women' means we have 2 women and 2 men

$$= \binom{4}{2} \times \binom{7}{2} = 6 \times 21 = 126$$

(ii) 'At least two women' means 2 women and 2 men **or** 3 women and 1 man **or** 4 women

2 women and 2 men

$$= \binom{4}{2} \times \binom{7}{2} = 6 \times 21 = 126$$

127

3 women and 1 man

$$= \binom{4}{3} \times \binom{7}{1} = 4 \times 7 = 28$$

4 women and 0 men $= \binom{4}{4} \times \binom{7}{0} = 1$

No. of delegations = 126 + 28 + 1 = 155.

(iii) 'At most 1 woman' means 0 women and 4 men **or** 1 woman and 3 men

0 women and 4 men

$$= \binom{4}{0} \times \binom{7}{4} = 1 \times 35 = 35$$

1 woman and 3 men

$$= \binom{4}{1} \times \binom{7}{3} = 4 \times 35 = 140$$

No. of delegations = 35 + 140 = 175.

Type 3

Points on a diagram

Example: How many triangles can be formed from 5 points, no 3 of which are collinear? If one point is the origin and this point must be used, then how many triangles can be formed?

Note: 'no 3 of which are collinear' means that there are only two points in a line but not 3.

Solution

We have 5 points but we need 3 to form a triangle, so from 5 points pick 3

$$\Rightarrow \binom{5}{3} = 10$$

If one point is used, we have from 4 points pick 2: $\binom{4}{2} = 6$.

Basic probability

The probability of a certain event, E, taking place, written as $P(E)$, is given by:

$$P(E) = \frac{\text{number of times E occurs}}{\text{number of times E could occur}}$$

Note 1: $0 \le P(E) \le 1$

Note 2: $P(E) = 0$ means E cannot happen.

$P(E) = 1$ means E is a certainty.

Note 3: $P(E \text{ does not happen}) = 1 - P(E \text{ does happen})$.

Note 4: 'Sample space' is the set of all possible outcomes of an experiment.

The Addition Rule / Or Rule

(a) If E and F are two events that cannot occur at the same time, then

$$P(E \text{ or } F) = P(E) + P(F)$$

(b) If E and F are two events that may occur at the same time, then

$$P(E \text{ or } F) = P(E) + P(F) - P(E \text{ with } F)$$

The Multiplication Rule / And Rule

$$P(E \text{ and } F) = P(E) \times P(F).$$

Method

> Read the question over and over.
> Find the total number of objects in the question.
> Try to write out in English what they have laid out in the question.
> Find answer by putting number of objects asked about in the question over the total number of objects.

Example: What is the probability of drawing a white marble from a bag with 4 white and 7 black marbles?

Solution

Total of 11 marbles, of which 4 are white.

$$P(\text{white ball}) = \frac{4}{11}$$

Example: A card is drawn from a pack at random. What is the probability that the card drawn is:

(i) a queen?
(ii) a spade?
(iii) a queen or a spade?

Solution

There are 52 cards in a pack (sample space is 52).

Total of 52 cards.

(i) $P(\text{queen}) = \frac{4}{52} = \frac{1}{13}$ since there are 4 queens in a pack of 52 cards.

(ii) $P(\text{spade}) = \frac{13}{52} = \frac{1}{4}$ since there are 13 spades in a pack of 52 cards.

(iii) $P(\text{queen or a spade})$
$= P(\text{queen}) + P(\text{spade}) - P(\text{queen or spade})$
$= \frac{4}{52} + \frac{13}{52} - \frac{1}{52} = \frac{16}{52} = \frac{4}{13}$

Example: In a class, there are 15 boys and 13 girls. Four of the boys wear glasses and three of the girls wear glasses. A pupil is picked at random from the class.

(i) What is the probability that the pupil is a boy?
(ii) What is the probability that the pupil wears glasses?
(iii) What is the probability that the pupil is a boy who wears glasses?

A girl is picked at random from the class.

(iv) What is the probability that she wears glasses?

Solution

28 in total: 15 boys, 13 girls

(i) Probability that the pupil is a boy: there are 15 boys and 28 people in total, so the probability of picking a boy = $\frac{15}{28}$

(ii) Probability that the pupil wears glasses: there are 7 people (4 boys and 3 girls) who wear glasses and 28 people in total, so the probability of glasses = $\frac{7}{28} = \frac{1}{4}$

(iii) Probability that the pupil is a boy who wears glasses: there are 4 boys who wear glasses in a total of 28, so probability of a boy who wears glasses = $\frac{4}{28} = \frac{1}{7}$

(iv) A girl is picked, so that means that we are now talking about only a total of 13 girls. Three of the girls wear glasses, so probability of a girl who wears glasses = $\frac{3}{13}$

Independent events

Example: In a bag containing 10 marbles, 4 are red and 6 are black. Find the probability that when a marble is taken out at random and replaced and a second marble is taken out:

(i) both were the same colour
(ii) one was red
(iii) at least one was red.

Solution

10 marbles in total, 4 of which are red. The marble is replaced, so that the outcome for the second event is the same.

(i) P(both same colour)

= P(both red) + P(both black)

P(both red) = $\frac{4}{10} \times \frac{4}{10} = \frac{4}{25}$

P(both black) = $\frac{6}{10} \times \frac{6}{10} = \frac{9}{25}$

P(all same colour) = $\frac{4}{25} + \frac{9}{25} = \frac{13}{25}$

(ii) P(one red) = $P(R) \times P(B)$

This answer must be multiplied by 2 as the red can be arranged in 2 ways, i.e. red black or black red.

P(one red) = $2\left(\frac{4}{10} \times \frac{6}{10}\right) = \frac{12}{25}$

(iii) $\boxed{P(\text{at least one red}) = 1 - P(\text{none red})}$

P(none red) = P(all black)

P(at least two red) = $1 - \frac{9}{25} = \frac{16}{25}$

Dependent events

Example: A bag contains 4 blue and 5 black discs. One disc is taken out and not replaced, and a second is taken out. Find the probability that:

(i) both were blue
(ii) the second one was blue
(iii) at least one was blue.

Solution

This time when we take a disc out it is not replaced, so that the probability changes for the second disc taken out.

(i) P(both blue) = P(blue) and P(blue) =

$\frac{4}{9} \times \frac{3}{8} = \frac{3}{18} = \frac{1}{6}$

(ii) The second blue: must write out the possible ways this can happen.

P(second one blue) = P(blue and blue) or P(black and blue)

P(blue and blue) = $\frac{4}{9} \times \frac{3}{8} = \frac{3}{18} = \frac{1}{6}$

P(black and blue) = $\frac{5}{9} \times \frac{4}{8} = \frac{5}{18}$

P(second one blue) = $\frac{3}{18} + \frac{5}{18} = \frac{5}{18} = \frac{4}{9}$

(iii) At least one blue

P(at least one blue) = $1 - P$(both black)

P(both black) = P(black) and P(black) =

$\frac{5}{9} \times \frac{4}{8} = \frac{5}{18}$

P(at least one blue) = $1 - \frac{5}{18} = \frac{13}{18}$

Birthday question

Example: Two people were asked, 'On what day of the week were you born?'
Find the probability that:

(i) both were born on Monday
(ii) both were born on the same day
(iii) both were born on different days.

Solution

(i) $P(\text{Mon and Mon}) = \frac{1}{7} \times \frac{1}{7} = \frac{1}{49}$

(ii) $P(\text{born and same}) = \frac{7}{7} \times \frac{1}{7} = \frac{1}{7}$

(iii) $P(\text{born on different days}) =$
$\frac{7}{7} \times \frac{6}{7} = \frac{6}{7}$

Note: In parts (ii) and (iii) the first person is born before we figure the rest out.

Sample Space

Example: If two unbiased dice are tossed, find the probability that:

(i) both dice show odd numbers
(ii) the sum of the results is 9 or greater.

Solution

This is an example of a sample space, where we write out all the possible answers.

```
11  21  31  41  51  61
12  22  32  42  52  62
13  23  33  43  53  63
14  24  34  44  54  64
15  25  35  45  55  65
16  26  36  46  56  66
```

(i) There are 36 answers and we have to count up the number of answers in which both are odd

11 31 51 13 33 53 15 35 55

Answer $\frac{9}{36} = \frac{1}{4}$

(ii) Find the results that add to 9 or more.

36 45 46 54 55 56 63 64 65 66

Answer $\frac{10}{36} = \frac{5}{18}$

131

Chapter 13
Statistics

This is one of the easier sections of the course and, as such, good revision here can pick you up a lot of marks.

Contents

(a) Mean – average (page 132)
(b) Weighted mean (page 137)
(c) To find the mode and median (page 138)
(d) To draw a histogram (page 139)
(e) To draw a cumulative frequency curve (page 140)
(f) Pie charts (page 141)
(g) Standard deviation (page 142).

Mean – average

The mean is the same as the average. The symbol used is $\bar{x}$.
There are 6 different types of question that have been asked here.

Type 1

To find the mean of a group of numbers

Example: Ann achieved the following results in her Christmas exams: 40% in English, 50% in Irish and 90% in maths. Find her mean mark.

Solution

This is very easy to do; just add the numbers up and divide by 3, since she did 3 exams:
We take this idea and apply it to a formula

$$\text{Mean} = \frac{\text{Add up the numbers}}{\text{Number of numbers}}$$

Example: Find the mean of 2, 4, 7, 3 and 1.

Solution

$$\text{Mean} = \frac{2+4+7+3+1}{5} = \frac{17}{5} = 3\frac{2}{5}$$

Note: Always show what you have done, no matter how easy.

Type 2

To find a missing number when given mean

Same type of question as the last one, but this time we start with different information.
Stick to the formula and method as done above. This time we are given the answer and must work back.

Example: If 3, 6, 8, x, 9 have a mean of 7, find the value of x.

Solution

$$\frac{3 + 6 + 8 + x + 9}{5} = 7$$

put the 7 over 1

$$\frac{26 + x}{5} = \frac{7}{1}$$

cross-mutiply

$$26 + x = 7(5)$$

multiply out

$$26 + x = 35$$

letters to one side, numbers to the other

$$x = 35 - 26$$

when a term crosses the equals sign it changes sign

$$x = 9$$

Note: x stands for an unknown number, so that is why we divided by 5.

Example: 2, 4, $2x$, $3x + 4$, 6, 7, 9 are a group of numbers that have a mean of 8. Find the value of x.

Solution

$$\frac{2 + 4 + 2x + 3x + 4 + 6 + 7 + 9}{7} = 8$$

$$\frac{32 + 5x}{7} = \frac{8}{1}$$

$$32 + 5x = 8(7)$$

$$32 + 5x = 56$$

$$5x = 24$$

$$x = \frac{24}{5} = 4.8$$

Note: $3x + 4$ is one number which consists of two parts.

Note: The answer does not have to be a whole number.

Type 3

To construct a frequency table and then find the mean

The next thing we move to is what is called a frequency table. This is a way of presenting information in a clear and quick way.

Look at the example below, which shows the number of goals scored in 20 games.

Number of goals	0 goals	1 goal	2 goals	3 goals	4 goals
Number of games	5	7	3	4	1

> The bottom figures show how often the event above them has occurred.

0 goals were scored in 5 games, 1 goal in 7 games, 2 goals in 3 games, 3 goals in 4 games and 4 goals in 1 game.

Sometimes we are asked questions that relate to the frequency table.

Example: Using the table below, answer the following:

(i) In how many games were there 3 goals scored?
(ii) How many games were there?
(iii) How many goals were scored in total?
(iv) How many games could have ended in a draw?

Goals	0	1	2	3	4	5
Games	3	6	4	5	0	2

Solution

(i) 3 goals were scored in 5 games.
(ii) To find the number of games add up the bottom. $3 + 6 + 4 + 5 + 0 + 2 = 20$

(iii) 3 games had 0 goals scored in each, so there must have been a total of 0 goals.

6 games had 1 goal scored in each, so there must have been a total of 6 goals.

4 games had 2 goals scored in each, so there must have been a total of 8 goals.

So to find the total number of goals scored, multiply the top by the bottom and add.

$(0 \times 3) + (1 \times 6) + (2 \times 4) + (3 \times 5) + (4 \times 0) + (5 \times 2)$

$= 0 + 6 + 8 + 15 + 0 + 10 = 39$

(iv) A draw means the score could be 0–0 (0 goals scored) or 1–1 (2 goals scored) or 2–2 (4 goals scored) and these results happened in $3 + 4 + 0 = 7$ games.

Note: $0 \times 3 = 0$; it is very easy to write down that $0 \times 3 = 3$, which is a very common mistake made.

Two methods could be used here to find the mean. Pick one and use it in all questions.

Method 1: Use the headings x, f, fx and then the formula:

$$\text{Mean} = \frac{\Sigma fx}{\Sigma f}$$

With the headings there are 3 lines.

Line 1: Under the x write the top line of the frequency table.
Line 2: Under the f write the bottom line of the frequency table.
Line 3: Under the fx multiply line 1 by line 2.

Notes: Σfx means add up line 3.
Σf means add up line 2.

Method 2:

$$\text{Mean} = \frac{\text{Top by bottom added}}{\text{Bottom added}}$$

To construct a frequency table

Example: Construct a frequency table for the following information, which shows the number of goals scored on the first day of the season and hence find the mean.

1 2 2 3 5 2
2 3 4 1 4 2

Solution

To form a frequency table simply count the number of 1s, 2s and so on.

Goals	1	2	3	4
Games	2	5	2	2

To find mean:

Method 1:
To find the mean, first make out a new table (make sure to learn the headings).

x	f	fx
1	2	2
2	5	10
3	2	6
4	2	8
Add	11	26

$$\text{Mean} = \frac{\Sigma fx}{\Sigma f} = \frac{26}{11}$$

Method 2:

$$\text{Mean} = \frac{\text{Top by bottom added}}{\text{Bottom added}}$$

$$\text{Mean} = \frac{(1\times 2)+(2\times 5)+(3\times 2)+(4\times 2)}{2+5+2+2}$$

$$= \frac{2+10+6+8}{11} = \frac{26}{11}$$

Type 4

To find the mean of a grouped frequency distribution table

A grouped frequency distribution table is where we group the information in wider bands. For example, we may talk about the number of children between the ages of 0 and 2.

> To find the mean we use the exact same method as above, but use the **mid-interval** of the group.

What is meant by mid-interval? What is the mid-interval of 0 and 2? The answer is the number in the middle of 0 and 2, so the mid-interval is 1. Mid-interval of 10 and 20 is 15.

Example: The following shows the ages of 30 children on a housing estate.

Age	0–2	2–4	4–6	6–8
No. of pupils	12	9	6	3

Use the table to find:

(i) the maximum number of children who could be under 3 years old
(ii) the maximum number of children who could be over 5 years old
(iii) the mean age.

Solution

(i) To find the maximum number who could be under 3 years old, we have to pay attention to 2 groups.

In the 0–2 group there are 12 children, all of whom must be under 3.
In the 2–4 group there are 9 children, all of whom could be under 3 for all we know, so the answer to the question is 12 + 9 = 21.

(ii) 'Over 5' means we have to look at the two groups where the chidren are over 5 or could be over 5. In the 6–8 group there are 3 children, who all must be over 5; and in the 4–6 group all 6 children could be over 5.
The answer is 6 + 3 = 9.

(iii) Mean

Method 1:

Interval	Mid-interval	f	fx
0–2	1	12	12
2–4	3	9	27
4–6	5	6	30
6–8	7	3	21
Add		30	90

$$\bar{x} = \frac{90}{30} = 3$$

Method 2:

$$= \frac{(1\times 12)+(3\times 9)+(5\times 6)+(7\times 3)}{12+9+6+3}$$

$$= \frac{12+27+30+21}{30} = \frac{90}{30} = 3$$

Type 5

To find a missing frequency when given mean

Same type of question as the last one, but this time we start with different information. Stick to the method.

Example: The table below shows the number of goals scored by a team during a season. If the mean number of goals scored is 2, find the value of x.

Goals	0	1	2	3	4
Games	3	3	4	x	3

Solution
Method 1:

x	f	fx
0	3	0
1	3	3
2	4	8
3	x	$3x$
4	3	12
Add	$13 + x$	$23 + 3x$

let answer = 2 from question

$$\frac{23 + 3x}{13 + x} = \frac{2}{1}$$

cross-multiply

$$23 + 3x = 2(13 + x)$$

multiply out

$$23 + 3x = 26 + 2x$$

letters to one side and numbers to the other

$$3x - 2x = 26 - 23$$
$$x = 3$$

Method 2:

$$\frac{\text{Top by bottom added}}{\text{Bottom added}}$$

$$\frac{(0 \times 3)+(1 \times 3)+(2 \times 4)+(3 \times x)+(4 \times 3)}{3 + 3 + 4 + x + 3} = 2$$

multiply out top and add bottom; let answer = 2 from question

$$\frac{0 + 3 + 8 + 3x + 12}{13 + x} = 2$$

tidy up top by adding

$$\frac{23 + 3x}{13 + x} = \frac{2}{1}$$

cross-multiply

$$23 + 3x = 2(13 + x)$$

multiply out

$$23 + 3x = 26 + 2x$$

letters to one side and numbers to the other

$$3x - 2x = 26 - 23$$
$$x = 3$$

Note: $0 + 3 + 8 + 3x + 12 = 23 + 3x$; this is where the most common mistake is made, and a lot of students will write $0 + 3 + 8 + 3x + 12 = 26x$, which is not correct.

Example: People attending a course were asked to choose one of the whole numbers from 1 to 12. The results were recorded as follows:

Number	1–3	4–6	7–9	10–12
No. of people	3	x	2	8

Using mid-interval values, 6.5 was calculated as the mean of the numbers chosen. Find the value of x.

Solution
Method 1:

Interval	Mid-interval	f	fx
1–3	2	3	6
4–6	5	x	$5x$
7–9	8	2	16
10–12	11	8	88
Add		$x + 13$	$5x + 110$

136

$$\frac{5x + 110}{x + 13} = 6.5$$

$$5x + 110 = 6.5(x + 13)$$

$$5x + 110 = 6.5x + 84.5$$

$$5x - 6.5x = 84.5 - 110$$

$$-1.5x = -25.5$$

$$x = 17$$

Method 2:

$$\frac{(2 \times 3) + (5 \times x) + (8 \times 2) + (11 \times 8)}{3 + x + 2 + 8} = 6.5$$

$$\frac{6 + 5x + 16 + 88}{x + 13} = 6.5$$

$$\frac{5x + 110}{x + 13} = 6.5$$

$$5x + 110 = 6.5(x + 13)$$

$$5x + 110 = 6.5x + 84.5$$

$$5x - 6.5x = 84.5 - 110$$

$$-1.5x = -25.5$$

$$x = 17$$

Type 6

Worded questions

These are questions in which we are told the number of numbers and their mean; what we have to do is find the sum of the numbers by using the idea that:

> Mean = $\frac{\text{sum of numbers}}{\text{number of numbers}}$
> and changing it around to
> Sum of numbers = mean × number of numbers

Example: The mean of 4 numbers is 6 and of another 5 numbers is 8. Find the mean of all 9 numbers.

Solution

4 numbers – mean of 6 – total of 24

5 numbers – mean of 8 – total of 40

We have figured out that there are 9 numbers which must have a total of 64 (24 + 40).

$$\text{Mean} = \frac{\text{sum of numbers}}{\text{number of numbers}} = \frac{64}{9}$$

Example: The mean age of 7 boys in a group is 13. When one of the boys leaves the group the mean age is decreased by 1. Find the age of the boy who left.

Solution

Number of boys × Mean age = Total

7 boys – mean age of 13 = total age of 91

6 boys – mean age of 12 = total age of 72

Age of boy who left = 91 – 72 = 19 years old.

Weighted mean

> Weighted mean = $\frac{\text{weights} \times \text{results added}}{\text{weights added}}$

Example: The table below shows the results obtained by a student in 3 exams. If the weights for Maths, English and Irish were 4:2:1 respectively, find the weighted average.

Subjects	Maths	English	Irish
Grades	70%	65%	55%

Solution

Weighted mean

$$= \frac{(4 \times 70) + (2 \times 65) + (1 \times 55)}{4 + 2 + 1}$$

$$= \frac{280 + 130 + 55}{7}$$

$$= \frac{465}{7} = 66.4$$

To find the mode and median

Mode – This is defined as the result that occurs most often, i.e. it is the result with the highest frequency. For a grouped frequency table it is called the **modal class** or **modal group**.

Median – the middle value, i.e. halfway. To find the median, write the numbers in order of size and find the halfway value.

Example: Find the mode and the median of 1, 3, 2, 4, 2, 3, 5, 2, 6.

Solution

Rewritten in order of size
= 1, 2, 2, 2, 3, 3, 4, 5, 6

The number that occurs most often is 2 (occurs 3 times), so it is the mode.

There are 9 numbers, so the median is in the centre which is the 5th number. The median is 3.

Example: Find the median of 2, 4, 6, 7, 3, 5

Solution

Rewritten in order of size = 2, 3, 4, 5, 6, 7

There are 6 numbers, so the median is in the centre which is between the 3rd and 4th numbers. The answer is 4.5.

Example: From the frequency table below, find:

(i) the mode
(ii) the median.

Goals	0	1	2	3	4	5
Games	3	6	4	5	0	2

Solution

(i) Mode is the event with the highest frequency. The answer is 1 goal because this happened 6 times, which is more than any other result.

(ii) There are 20 games in total and we need to find the median. We need to find what was scored in the 10th and 11th games.
The first 3 games had 0 goals scored and the next 6 games had 1 goal scored, so that accounts for the first 9 games. The 10th and 11th games must be in the next group where there were 2 goals scored, so the median must be 2.

Example: The following shows the heights of 30 pupils in a school. Find:

(i) the modal group
(ii) the interval in which the median lies.

Height	0–2	2–4	4–6	6–8
No. of pupils	12	9	6	3

Solution

(i) The modal group is the group with the highest number on the bottom (the highest frequency). The answer to this question is that the modal group is 0–2.

(ii) If there are 30 pupils, then the median height must be between the 15th and 16th pupils. The first 12 pupils are in the 0–2 group. The next 9 pupils are in the 2–4 group, which would bring us up to 21 pupils, so the 15th and 16th pupils are in the 0–2 group. Therefore the median interval must be 0–2.

To draw a histogram

When dealing with the diagrams that follow always remember that the frequency is on the vertical axis of the diagram. An easy way to remember this is that the top of the table goes on the bottom of the diagram, and the figures on the bottom go up the side of the diagram.

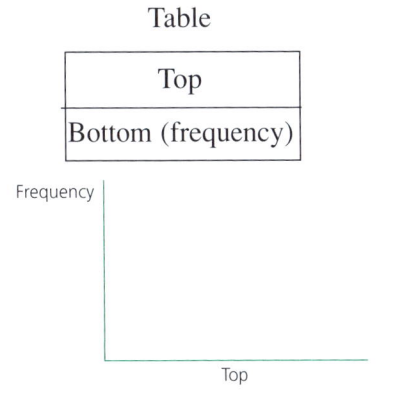

Table

Top
Bottom (frequency)

Frequency

Top

The area of each rectangle represents the frequency.

Example: At a sports meeting, the distances for competitors each throwing a javelin are:

Distance	0–20	20–50	50–60	60–80	80–120
No. of competitors	8	21	8	10	24

Show this information in a histogram.

Solution

First make out a new table for yourself using the following.

(i) Write all the gaps on top of the frequency table.
(ii) Find the smallest gap, 50–60, and let this represent a unit of 1.
(iii) Adjust all other gaps accordingly i.e. 0–20 = gap of 20 = 2 units, 20–50 = gap of 30 = 3 units, 60–80 = gap of 20 = 2 units, 80–120 = gap of 40 = 4 units. These we call our base.
(iv) *Divide* each frequency by new base to find actual height up.

Gap	20	30	10	20	40	
Distance	0–20	20–50	50–60	60–80	80–120	← Bottom
No. of competitors	8	21	8	10	24	
Base	2	3	1	2	4	
Height	4	7	8	5	6	← Side

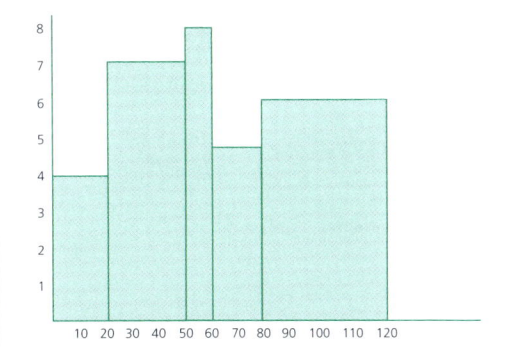

To find the frequency of a grouped frequency table when given the histogram

Example: The histogram shows the ages of a group of people. What was the modal class?

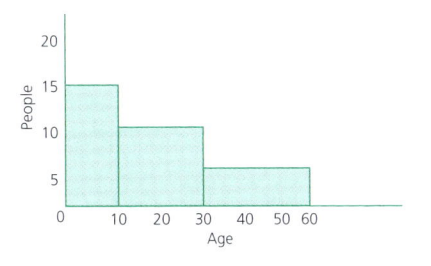

Solution

Draw out a grouped frequency table.

Remember that:

(a) what is on the horizontal axis is our groups, i.e. 0–10, 10–30, 30–60. Fill this in on the table first.
(b) what is on the vertical axis is the actual heights up (not the frequency). Fill this in on the table.
(c) Find the smallest interval: 0–10
Let this represent a unit of 1.
Adjust all other intervals accordingly, i.e. 10–30 = 2 units, 30–60 = 3 units.
Multiply base by height to find the frequency.

Age	0–10	10–30	30–60
People	15	20	15
Base	1	2	3
Height	15	10	5

The modal class is 10–30.

To draw a cumulative frequency curve (ogive)

Example: Draw a cumulative frequency graph (ogive) to represent the following information, which shows the marks obtained by 100 students in a maths exam.

Marks	0–10	10–20	20–30	30–40	40–50	50–60	60–70
Students	10	2	5	10	41	28	4

Use the graph to find:

(a) the median mark
(b) the interquartile range
(c) the number of students who obtained over 56 marks.

Solution

We must first draw a cumulative frequency table. Remember to **ADD**.

Marks	<10	<20	<30	<40	<50	<60	<70
Students	10	12	17	27	68	96	100

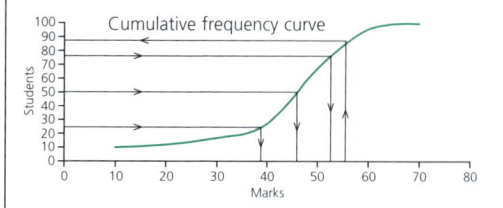

Cumulative frequency curve

(a) Median – this is half of the total frequency. We always start halfway up the vertical axis, draw a line straight across until it hits the curve and then come down to find the answer. Answer 46.
(b) Interquartile range – this is between the first quarter and the third quarter of the total frequency: i.e. start at 25 and 75 on the vertical axis, come across to hit the graph, and then come straight down for the interquartile range. Answer 52 – 39 = 13.
(c) We have to decide which axis to start from. This very much depends on the information given in the question, so read it carefully.

In this question we were given the students' marks and asked to find the number of students.
Start on the horizontal axis at 56, go up to hit the graph. We come up with a value of 88. The question asked us to find the number of people who scored *over* 56, so we have to take the answer we got away from the total number of students. Answer = 100 – 88 = 12.

Note: We are allowed an error of ± 3.

Example: From the cumulative frequency table, fill in the frequency distribution table.

Age	<2	<4	<6	<8	<10
No. of people	3	7	15	19	20

Solution

To fill in the frequency table just SUBTRACT.

Age	0–2	2–4	4–6	6–8	8–10
No. of people	3	4	8	4	1

Pie charts

Example: The numbers of goals scored in 20 matches were as follows. Draw a pie chart.

No. of goals	0	1	2	3	4
No. of games	6	2	4	5	3

Solution

If we are asked to draw a pie chart we must:

(a) find the total number of games (add up the bottom)

$6 + 2 + 4 + 5 + 3 = 20$

(b) find the angle for each game by using

$$\text{Angle} = \frac{\text{no. of games}}{\text{total}} \times \frac{360}{1}$$

0 goals = $\frac{6}{20} \times \frac{360}{1} = 108°$

1 goal = $\frac{2}{20} \times \frac{360}{1} = 36°$

2 goals = $\frac{4}{20} \times \frac{360}{1} = 72°$

3 goals = $\frac{5}{20} \times \frac{360}{1} = 90°$

4 goals = $\frac{3}{20} \times \frac{360}{1} = 54°$

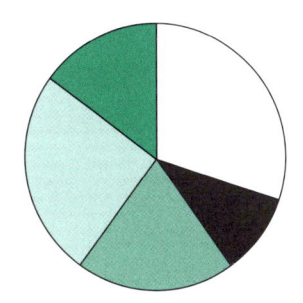

Sometimes we are given the pie chart.

$$\text{Number required} = \frac{\text{Angle}}{360} \times \frac{\text{Total}}{1}$$

Example: A survey of 18 people was taken to find the colours they prefer. The results are shown in the pie chart below. Find the number of people in each group.

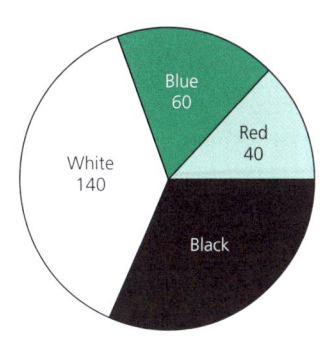

Solution

White: $\frac{140}{360} \times \frac{18}{1} = 7$

Blue: $\frac{60}{360} \times \frac{18}{1} = 3$

Red: $\frac{40}{360} \times \frac{18}{1} = 2$

Black = $\frac{120}{360} \times \frac{18}{1} = 6$

Standard deviation

There are two types of question that can be asked here.

Note: The symbol for standard deviation is σ (Greek *sigma*).

Type 1

To find the standard deviation of a set of numbers

Method:

Step 1:	Find the mean.
Step 2:	Write down your headings and follow them.
Step 3:	Write down the formula, put figures in and work out using a calculator.

Headings to learn: $x, x - \bar{x}, (x - \bar{x})^2$

Formula to learn:

Standard deviation $\sigma = \sqrt{\dfrac{\Sigma(x - \bar{x})^2}{n}}$, where n is the number of numbers.

Example: Find the standard deviation of 3, 6, 7, 10, 14.

Solution

$\bar{x} = \dfrac{3 + 6 + 7 + 10 + 14}{5} = 8$

x	$x - \bar{x}$	$(x - \bar{x})^2$
3	−5	25
6	−2	4
7	−1	1
10	2	4
14	6	36
		70

$\sigma = \sqrt{\dfrac{\Sigma(x - \bar{x})^2}{n}}$, where n is the number of numbers.

$\sigma = \sqrt{\dfrac{70}{5}} = \sqrt{14} = 3.74$

Type 2

To find the standard deviation of a frequency table

Method:

Step 1:	Find the mean.
Step 2:	Write down your headings and follow them.
Step 3:	Write down the formula, put figures in and work out using a calculator.

Headings to learn:

$x, f, x - \bar{x}, (x - \bar{x})^2 \ \ f(x - \bar{x})^2$

Formula to learn: Standard deviation

$= \sigma = \sqrt{\dfrac{\Sigma f(x - \bar{x})^2}{\Sigma f}}$

Example: Find the standard deviation to one decimal place from the following information:

Height	2–4	4–6	6–8	8–10
No of pupils	6	9	4	1

Solution

x is the top line of the frequency table (use mid-intervals).

f is the bottom line of the frequency table

142

xf multiply the first two lines

$x - \bar{x}$ from each *x* subtract the mean

$(x - \bar{x})^2$ square the last line

$f(x - \bar{x})^2$ multiply the second line by the fifth line

x	f	xf	$x - \bar{x}$	$(x - \bar{x})^2$	$f(x - \bar{x})^2$
3	6	18	−2	4	24
5	9	45	0	0	0
7	4	28	2	4	16
9	1	9	4	16	16
Add	20	100			56

$$\bar{x} = \frac{\Sigma fx}{\Sigma f} = \frac{100}{20} = 5$$

$$\sigma = \sqrt{\frac{\Sigma f(x - \bar{x})^2}{\Sigma f}}$$

$$= \sqrt{\frac{56}{20}} = \sqrt{2.8} = 1.67$$

$$= 1.7 \text{ to one decimal place}$$

Chapter 14
Linear Programming

Contents:

(i)   Inequalities (page 144)
(ii) (a) parts (page 144)
(iii) (b) parts (page 146).

Inequalities

There are two types of inequality sign that we are going to see in these questions.

| $\leq$ means less than or equal to. |
| $\geq$ means greater than or equal to. |

(a) parts

There are 3 different types of (a) part that have been asked.

The main idea here is to be able to draw a line, as done in the line notes.

Two regions to have learnt off by heart:

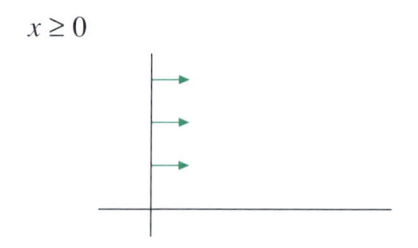

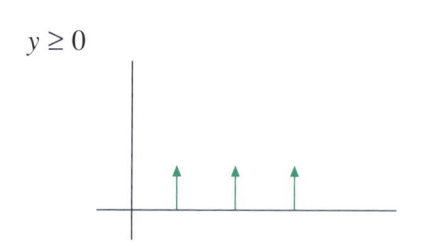

$x \geq 0$

$y \geq 0$

Type 1

Example: State 3 regions shown by the diagram below.

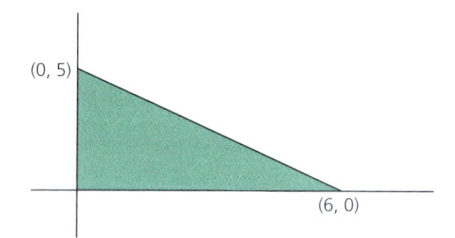

(0, 5)

(6, 0)

Solution

The first thing you must do yourself is put arrows on the diagram. Can you see which way the arrows must go in order to represent the shaded region? The shaded region is contained inside the triangle, so that the arrows must come from the sides of the triangle and face inwards.

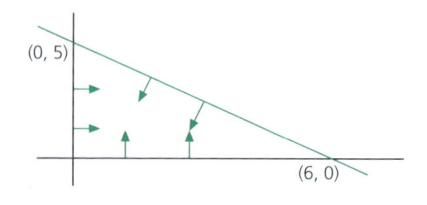

(0, 5)

(6, 0)

Note: When you draw one of these out it does not have to be a work of art; you are just trying to get the arrow going in the correct direction.

The first two are the easy ones above, of $x \geq 0$ and $y \geq 0$, because we have learnt them.

It is the third one we must find. The first thing we need to do is find the equation of the line between the points (0, 5) and (6, 0).

First we must find the slope of (0, 5) to (6, 0):

$$(0, 5) \text{ and } (6, 0)$$
$$x_1, y_1 \qquad x_2, y_2$$

use the given points in the slope formula

$$m = \frac{y_2 - y_1}{x_2 - x_1}$$

put figures in, tidy up and put minus on top

$$m = \frac{0 - 5}{6 - 0} = \frac{-5}{6}$$

Use the equation-of-a-line formula with either point and $m = \frac{-5}{6}$

$$y - y_1 = m(x - x_1)$$
$$y - 5 = -\frac{5}{6}(x - 0)$$

cross-multiply by the bottom

$$6(y - 5) = -5x$$

multiply out to have no brackets left

$$6y - 30 = -5x$$

bring the letters to the left and the numbers to the right

$$5x + 6y = 30$$

(remember if a term crosses the equals sign it changes sign)

Now we need to put in an inequality sign. We can explain the inequalities by subbing (0, 0) into the equations.

Sub in $x = 0$ and $y = 0$ into the equation $5x + 6y = 30$.

$6(0) + 5(0) = 0$ since 0 is less than 30 then we must use the < sign

Answers are $x \geq 0$ and $y \geq 0$ and $5x + 6y \leq 30$.

Type 2

Example: Plot on a diagram the region bounded by the lines:

$$x \geq 0$$
$$y \geq 0$$
$$x + 2y \leq 4$$

Solution

The first two you should be able to do from above, and even if you only do these two out you will pick up some marks.

To draw out the third one, we first ignore the inequality sign and draw as if a line.

Draw the line $x + 2y = 4$ by finding where it cuts the x- and y-axes.

On the x-axis the value of $y = 0$; in real terms this means the x-term has gone

$$2y = 4 \qquad \text{divide by 2}$$
$$y = 2$$

You must remember that every point is set up in the same way, with the x-value first followed by the y-value.

One point is (0, 2).

On the y-axis the value of $x = 0$; in real terms the y-term has gone.

$$x = 4$$

Other point is (4, 0).

Which way the arrows go on the line is the only issue. Sub $x = 0$ and $y = 0$ into the equation $x + 2y = 4$.

$(0) + 2(0) = 0 < 4$ since 0 is less than 4, then the arrow faces in towards $(0, 0)$.

Note: We could have put in any number, but $(0, 0)$ is the most convenient. If the line we have to draw goes through the origin, then pick any other point, like $(1, 0)$.

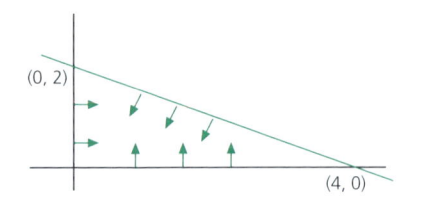

Type 3

Example:

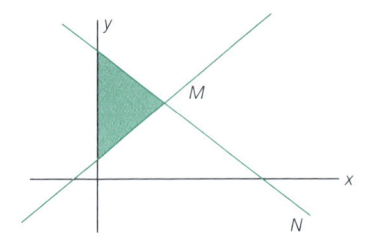

The equation of the line M is $x - y + 1 = 0$ and the equation of the line N is $x + y - 6 = 0$.

Write down the three inequalities that define the triangular region in the diagram.

Solution

First thing do is to put the arrows in the right direction.

$x \geq 0$ from above

M is $x - y + 1 = 0$, so we need to put in a point to see which inequality sign we will use. We sub in the point $(0, 0)$, but since the arrows are not facing this point we will use the opposite inequality sign in our answer.

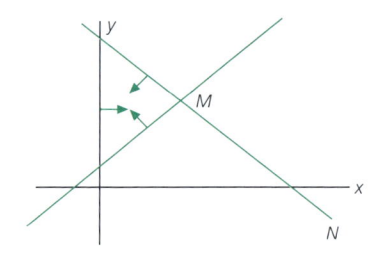

Sub $x = 0$ and $y = 0$ into the equation $x - y + 1 = 0$.

$0 - 0 + 1 = 1 > 0$, but because the arrows face away from this point we are going to use $<$ in our answer.

Answer: $x - y + 1 \leq 0$

N is $x + y - 6 = 0$; sub in the point $(0, 0)$. Since the arrows are facing this point we will use an inequality sign and get:

$$0 + 0 - 6 = -6 < 0$$

Answer: $x + y - 6 \leq 0$

Three inequalities are $x \geq 0$, $x - y + 1 \leq 0$ and $x + y - 6 \leq 0$.

(b) parts

> We need 2 inequalities, which requires converting English into Maths.
> Show the inequalities on a diagram and shade in a region.
> Use simultaneous equations to find the point of intersection.
> Draw out a table for the maximum part of the question.

- You must read the question over and over again in an attempt to come up with two inequalities.
- Read it once without writing anything down.
- Read it a second time; see what two objects they are on about.
- Write down 2 inequalities. Read it once more to see whether what you have written makes sense.

Note: The way the question is written is often the key to the answer. They either split the question up so that each section contains one inequality, or they have an inequality in a sentence.

Note: The questions so far have given us information about:

(i) area
(ii) money
(iii) work days
(iv) time.

Example: A farmer has not more than 2,000 m² of ground for planting apple trees and blackcurrant bushes. The ground space required for an apple tree is 50 m² and for a blackcurrant bush is 5m².

The planting of an apple tree costs €20 and the planting of a blackcurrant bush costs €4.

The farmer has at most €1,000 to spend on planting.

If the farmer plants x apple trees and y blackcurrant bushes, write down two inequalities in x and y and illustrate these on graph paper.

When fully grown, each apple tree will produce a crop worth €90 and each blackcurrant bush a crop worth €15.

How many of each should be planted so that the farmer's gross income is a maximum? Calculate the farmer's maximum profit.

Solution

In this question we are told about two separate things, namely area covered and money (cost of planting). We try to come up with two inequalities based on these pieces of information.

You must do one at a time, so read each statement over and over again.

'A farmer has not more than 2,000 m² of ground for planting apple trees and blackcurrant bushes. The ground space required for an apple tree is 50 m² and for a blackcurrant bush is 5 m².'

'Not more than 2,000' means must be less than or equal to 2,000, in maths written as ≤ 2000 (if in doubt use the less than $<$ sign).

Each apple tree x requires 50 m², so total area under apples must be the number of apples by the space required per apple = $50x$.

Each blackcurrant bush y requires 5 m², so total area under blackcurrant bushes must be the number of blackcurrant bushes by the space required per bush = $5y$.

Put together all the information above to come up with the inequality:

$50x + 5y \leq 2000$ we can make life easier if we divide across by 5

$10x + y \leq 400$

Note: It is very easy to make silly mistakes with the figures (like writing down 200 instead of 2,000, or you divide across by 5 incorrectly), which will not cost you a lot of marks but will make the rest of the question more difficult.

'The planting of an apple tree costs €20 and the planting of a blackcurrant bush costs €4.

The farmer has at most €1,000 to spend on planting.'

'Not more than €1,000' means must be less than or equal to 1,000, in maths written as ≤ 1000.

Each apple tree x cost €20, so total cost of the apple trees must be the number of apple trees by the cost per tree = $20x$.

Each blackcurrant bush y cost €4, so total cost of blackcurrant bushes must be the number of blackcurrant bushes by the cost per bush = $4y$.

Put together all the information above to come up with the inequality:

$20x + 4y ≤ 1000$ we can make life easier if we divide across by 4

$5x + y ≤ 250$

Now we have two inequalities that we can show on the one diagram:

$$10x + y ≤ 400$$

Ignore the inequality, so draw $10x + y = 400$.

On x-axis $y = 0$

$$10x = 400$$
$$x = 40$$

One point is (40, 0).

On y-axis $x = 0$

$$y = 400$$

Other point is (0, 400).

$$5x + y ≤ 250$$

Ignore the inequality, so draw $5x + y = 250$.

On x-axis $y = 0$

$$5x = 250$$
$$x = 50$$

One point is (50, 0).

On y-axis $x = 0$

$$y = 250$$

Other point is (0, 250).

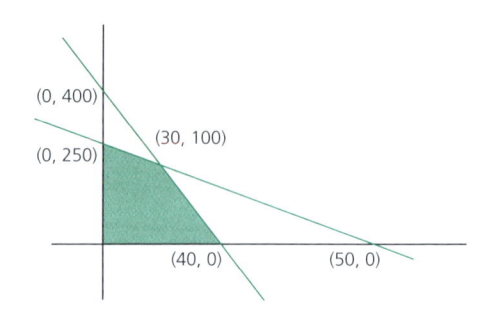

If we were to put an arrow on each line then the arrows would face in on each line, so we come up with the shaded region as above.

Even though we are not asked, the next thing to find is the point of intersection using simultaneous equations. Again we can forget about the inequality signs:

$$10x + y = 400$$
$$5x + y = 250$$

Change the sign of the bottom line and add.

$$10x + y = 400$$
$$-5x - y = -250$$

$$5x = 150 \text{ divide across by 5}$$
$$x = 30$$

Sub $x = 30$ into the first equation:

$$10(30) + y = 400$$

replace the x with 30 and multiply out

$$300 + y = 400$$

leave letters on left, numbers on right

$$y = 100$$

So point of intersection is (30, 100).

We have answered the first part of the question in that we have come up with two inequalities and have shown them on a graph, but now we must answer what is known as the maximum part of the question.

When fully grown, each apple tree will produce a crop worth €90 and each blackcurrant bush a crop worth €15.

How many of each should be planted so that the farmer's gross income is a maximum?

Calculate the farmer's maximum profit.

From your diagram use the 3 points that determine the shaded area: (0, 250), (30, 100) and (40, 0), and come up with a table from the information given.

Points	$90x + 15y$	Total
(0, 250)	90(0) + 15(250)	3,750
(30, 100)	90(30) + 15(100)	4,200
(40, 0)	90(40) + 15(0)	3,600

The farmer should plant 30 apple trees and 100 blackcurrant bushes for maximum income.

The maximum profit is €4,200.

Example: A parking lot has an area of 1,500 m². The parking area required for a car is 15 m² and for a bus is 60 m². Not more than 46 vehicles can be accommodated at any time.

If x represents the number of cars and y represents the number of buses parked, write two inequalities in x and y.

Solution

This is a harder question because it seems as if they have told us about only one thing, namely area.

A parking lot has an area of 1,500 m². The parking area required for a car is 15 m² and for a bus is 60 m².

'A parking lot has an area of 1,500 m²' means area used must be less than or equal to 1500, in maths written as ≤ 1500.

Each car x needs 15 m², so total space for cars = $15x$.

Each bus y needs 60 m², so total space for buses = $60x$.

Put together all the information above to come up with the inequality:

$$15x + 60y \leq 1500 \quad \text{divide by 15}$$

$$x + 4y \leq 100$$

If we look at the next line after the information on area, we are told that 'Not more than 46 vehicles can be accommodated at any time.'

What does this mean?

We have x cars and y buses and at most 46 vehicles, so

$$x + y \leq 46$$

We now have 2 inequalities, which we could show on a diagram and answer a maximum question if asked.

149